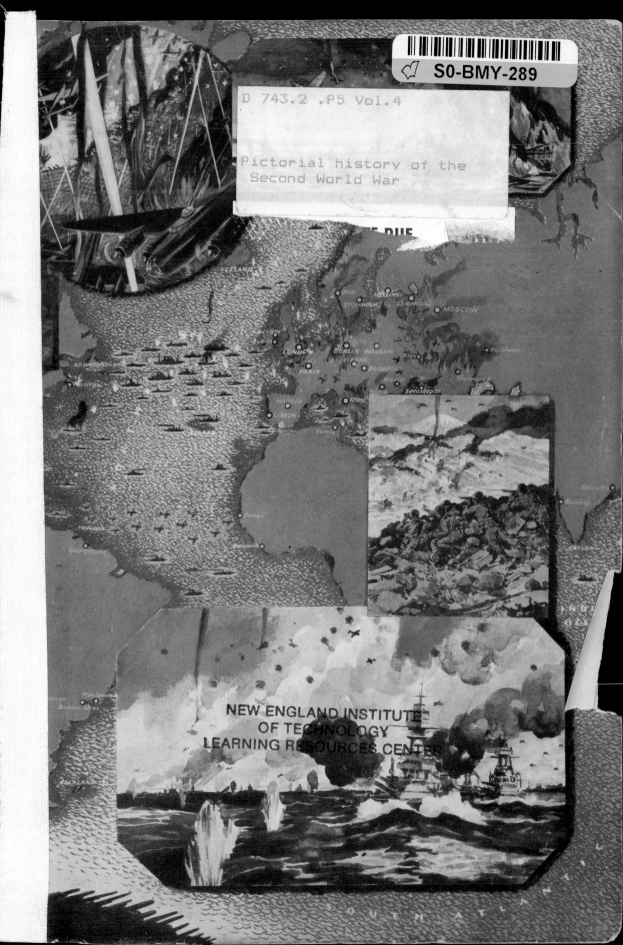

Pictorial history of the
Second World War

PICTORIAL HISTORY

OF THE

SECOND WORLD WAR

A PHOTOGRAPHIC RECORD
OF ALL THEATERS OF ACTION
CHRONOLOGICALLY ARRANGED

VOL. 4

New York
WM. H. WISE and CO., INC.
1946

CONTENTS

THE SIXTH YEAR

ACKNOWLEDGMENTS

Photographs in this publication were obtained from the following sources:

British Information Service — 1551, 1580, 1587, 1598, 1632, 1650, 1654, 1660, 1661, 1664, 1665, 1668, 1689, 1706, 1716, 1726, 1739, 1743, 1930, 1933, 1939, 1941, 1956

French Press and Information Service — 1565, 1566, 1567, 1638, 1649, 1663, 1710, 1738

International News Photo — 1550, 1553, 1593, 1602, 1603, 1604, 1628, 1629, 1639, 1645, 1652, 1653, 1674, 1675, 1676, 1677, 1678, 1707, 1709, 1712, 1720, 1723, 1727, 1748, 1749, 1757, 1760, 1782, 1796, 1800, 1801, 1812, 1840

Netherlands Information Bureau — 1631, 1632, 1925

New York News — 1884

Odhams Press — 1568, 1577, 1589, 1594, 1595, 1596, 1597, 1600, 1605, 1607, 1612, 1613, 1620, 1622, 1623, 1625, 1626, 1627, 1633, 1634, 1667, 1681, 1900, 1901, 1915, 1952, 1980, 1991, 2011

Official Coast Guard Photo — 1608, 1609, 1610, 1611, 1772, 1773, 1775

Office of Inter-American Affairs — 1799

Official U. S. Marine Corps Photo — 1576, 1578, 1658, 1769, 1771, 1774, 1776, 1777, 1789, 1858, 1859, 1860, 1871, 1881, 1894, 1896, 1966, 1969, 1975, 1977, 1986, 1990, 1993, 1995, 1999

Official U. S. Navy Photo — 1562, 1563, 1570, 1599, 1614, 1615, 1616, 1617, 1618, 1621, 1642, 1643, 1656, 1657, 1704, 1705, 1724, 1759, 1764, 1765, 1766, 1767, 1770, 1785, 1809, 1816, 1817, 1830, 1849, 1870, 1872, 1873, 1895, 1917, 1943, 1958, 1959, 1960, 1961, 1963, 1979, 1989, 1992, 1994, 2002, 2004, 2007, 2012, 2013, 2014, 2030, 2041

Press Association — 1545, 1547, 1548, 1549, 1552, 1554, 1555, 1558, 1560, 1569, 1582, 1583, 1584, 1585, 1586, 1602, 1607, 1624, 1637, 1639, 1648, 1651, 1653, 1655, 1666, 1670, 1679, 1682, 1683, 1685, 1686, 1687, 1688, 1690, 1691, 1692, 1693, 1694, 1695, 1696, 1698, 1699, 1701, 1702, 1703, 1706, 1708, 1731, 1739, 1741, 1745, 1753, 1761, 1778, 1781, 1784, 1798, 1802, 1803, 1804, 1807, 1820, 1821, 1826, 1827, 1829, 1835, 1836, 1837, 1843, 1844, 1845, 1847, 1850, 1853, 1856, 1861, 1865, 1867, 1868, 1874, 1876, 1877, 1879, 1882, 1883, 1886, 1887, 1890, 1891, 1897, 1898, 1899, 1903, 1904, 1905, 1912, 1914, 1919, 1920, 1921, 1922, 1923, 1924, 1927, 1928, 1929, 1932, 1937, 1944, 1945, 1946, 1947, 1948, 1949, 1950, 1951, 1954, 1955, 1957, 1965, 1970, 1971, 1973, 1974, 1976, 1982, 1983, 1984, 1987, 1988, 1996, 1997, 1998, 2000, 2002, 2003, 2005, 2006, 2008, 2009, 2010, 2016, 2017, 2018, 2019, 2020, 2021, 2022, 2023, 2025, 2026, 2027, 2028, 2029, 2031, 2032, 2033, 2034, 2035, 2038, 2039, 2040, 2042, 2043, 2044, 2045

Sovfoto — 1571, 1588, 1591, 1601, 1640, 1669, 1672, 1673, 1697, 1715, 1717, 1718, 1719, 1721, 1722, 1725, 1729, 1730, 1734, 1737, 1740, 1742, 1744, 1751, 1781, 1783, 1808, 1818, 1824, 1851, 1854, 1855, 1875, 1902, 1907, 1913, 1916, 1934, 1935, 1936, 2024, 2036, 2037

U. S. Army Air Forces — 1561, 1572, 1573, 1635, 1641, 1736, 1746, 1750, 1763, 1787, 1788, 1814, 1832, 1833, 1848, 1909, 1931, 1953, 1967, 1968, 1978, 1991, 2011, 2015

U. S. Army Signal Corps Photo — 1546, 1556, 1557, 1559, 1564, 1590, 1592, 1606, 1630, 1644, 1645, 1646, 1647, 1659, 1662, 1680, 1701, 1711, 1713, 1728, 1731, 1732, 1733, 1735, 1754, 1755, 1756, 1758, 1762, 1779, 1780, 1786, 1790, 1791, 1797, 1804, 1805, 1806, 1807, 1810, 1811, 1813, 1815, 1825, 1831, 1834, 1841, 1842, 1846, 1852, 1862, 1863, 1864, 1866, 1869, 1878, 1880, 1888, 1889, 1892, 1893, 1894, 1904, 1906, 1908, 1915, 1926, 1938, 1940, 1942, 1944, 1945, 1946, 1953, 1962, 1964, 1968, 1972, 1977, 2001, 2008

Yank, the Army Weekly — 1700 and 1714 by Sgt. Richardson, 1752 by Sgt. Hanley, 1822 by Sgt. Richardson, 1823 by Sgt. Peters, 1828 by Pfc. Coffey, 1839 by Sgt. Peters

FOREWORD

THIS fourth volume of the PICTORIAL HISTORY OF THE SECOND WORLD WAR dramatically pictures the sensational events leading to the complete defeat of Germany and Japan and vividly portrays the memorable and history-making scenes at the surrender ceremonies.

The battle for Germany is here completely documented by photographs. The reader actually sees the spectacular crossing of the Rhine and the break-up of the inner Reich as the Allies overrun it. The great Russian offensive is shown in stirring pictures from Warsaw to Berlin. The whole amazing story of horror and loot uncovered in Germany is revealed in pictures that cannot be refuted.

The final debacle in the Pacific is perhaps even more dramatic than the crushing of Nazi Germany. The awe-inspiring advent of the atomic bomb brought an entirely new element into the war. The actual bursts of the two bombs dropped on Japan are pictured as well as the damage done. The beginning of a new era is told in eloquent photographs.

Although the global war had reached vast proportions in the sixth year, no important aspect of the war is omitted. Events in the Pacific, Burma, China and Borneo, events in Italy and Greece are all faithfully recorded as well as important political happenings closely related to the war such as the death of President Franklin Delano Roosevelt, the grisly end of Mussolini, and the rise to power of Britain's Clement Attlee.

The main emphasis of the book, however, remains on the actual battlefronts where scores of photographers gave their lives to record the drama of life and death at close quarters with the enemy. Official Army, Navy and Air Force photographers as well as news cameramen have provided voluminous records from which the reader is enabled to see what actually occurred on the blood drenched battlefields, in the air, and at sea. The reader is given a combat view of the War.

The distribution of space has been determined by the unequalled importance of events. After victory in Europe a relatively small number of pictures tells the story in the Pacific until the final rush of events when a larger number of pictures is included to give the full story of final victory.

THE PUBLISHERS

SEPTEMBER - FEBRUARY

THE Battle of France had become a rout in September with the Allied armies chasing the Nazis towards their homeland, or leaving them in rear area pockets to be mopped up later. The British took Ghent and the United States First Army won Sedan on September 7, while American forces in southern France were rapidly pushing up the Rhone Valley, capturing Lyon on September 5 and establishing contact with the American Third Army on September 11. The next day German soil was entered for the first time, north of Trier, by the United States First Army.

A bold bid to turn the Siegfried Line and end the Battle of Germany at a stroke was made on September 17 when the Allies landed an airborne army on the Rhine Delta near Nijmegen and Eindhoven. The coup failed when all but 2,000 of 8,000 sky troops were wiped out. The Allied armies were forced to pause at the Reich's border while supplies and reinforcements were brought up.

The Western Front stirred anew in mid-November when six Allied armies pressed a large scale offensive to clear the Nazis from the area west of the Rhine. On November 17 more than 2,350 American and British bombers, in the biggest tactical supporting operation of the war, coordinated with the ground forces. Metz, Belfort, and Saarebourg went down under the attack but the drive fell short of its major objective.

On December 16 Field Marshal Karl von Rundstedt surprised the First Army's Belgian and Luxembourg defenses with a counter offensive which opened a gap 60 miles wide and drove a wedge 50 miles deep into the American lines. The Yanks held firm on the Nazi flanks, however, and were able gradually to strangle the German drive with powerful attacks from north and south. The Germans failed to gain for the first time on December 28 and the massive offensive came to a halt. Later it was announced that Allied casualties in December on all fronts in western Europe totaled 74,788.

Throughout January the Nazi's tried frantically to extricate themselves from the Belgian Bulge. They abandoned nearly 100 square miles of their untenable position and furious Allied air attacks on January 21 and 22 wrecked or damaged nearly 7,000 Nazi vehicles fleeing toward the safety of the Siegfried Line. Early in the month the Germans had attempted to balance the defeat with an attack in the Saar region but this too was frustrated and by February the Allied Armies were again feeling their way into the Siegfried defenses.

On February 2 the Yanks entered Colmar and on February 12 Pruem was captured. By the middle of the month Canadian, British and American forces were engaged in the long awaited full-scale offensive for the Rhine.

THE RUSSIAN FRONT

IN the fall and early winter Russian forces were still at the gates of Warsaw and Stalin set himself the task of liquidating the Nazi satellites in the Balkans and along the Baltic Sea. Hostilities with Finland ceased on September 5; Tallinn, capital of Estonia, was captured on September 22; and on October 13 the Latvian capital of Riga was conquered.

In the Balkans Stalin's forces moved across the Czechoslovakian and Hungarian borders on September 24 and by October 20 other units had advanced to Yugoslavia where they occupied the capital, Belgrade. Bulgaria signed an Armistice with the United Nations on October 28. Budapest, Hungary's capital, was completely encircled by December 26 and the Russians swung towards Vienna. Hungary's final capitulation came on January 21.

Their flanks secure, the Russian Armies broke the stalemate in Poland January 12 with a new offensive of unprecedented magnitude along the entire 600 mile front from the Baltic to Budapest. Sweeping forward between Cracow and Warsaw the Russians shattered the German lines, seizing Radom on January 16, and the following day liberating long-besieged Warsaw. Unchecked, the Soviet drive poured with lightning speed into German Silesia and by January 28 the Dabrowa coal fields and industries were in Russian hands. On January 24 Oppeln, bulwark of Upper Silesia, was conquered.

Other powerful drives to the north overcame all opposition with incredible speed, penetrating East Prussia to capture the fortress city of Tannenberg January 21 and seizing Insterburg and Allenstein the following day. Simultaneously campaigns were waged in Lithuania where Memel fell on January 28, and in East Pomerania where a 30 mile front was established.

By February 1 Soviet forces had forged a continuous line within Germany extending 395 miles from southern Silesia to the Polish Corridor. Moscow stated that 295,000 Germans were killed and 86,000 captured in the first 15 days of the great offensive. And in 23 days of fighting, Marshal Gregory K. Zhukov's First White Russian Army had advanced 280 miles from Warsaw to the Oder River, taking Zellin, 33 miles from Berlin, and gravely menacing Frankfort and Kuestrin, the last citadels on the direct road to the German capital.

STALEMATE IN ITALY

THE British Eighth and the American Fifth Army began an assault in September on the Gothic Line in Italy, about 100 miles north of Rome. The Eighth Army succeeded in taking Rimini, eastern anchor of the Gothic Line, on September 21, and the Fifth Army broke the stubborn defense of Futa Pass on September 23. The Gothic Line was thereby penetrated but the Germans stiffened their resistance and progress of the Allies became slow and costly.

Another offensive in the Mediterranean was launched in Greece, which the British invaded September 26. Here the battle against the Nazis was complicated by civil war and Prime Minister Churchill found it necessary to go to Athens and set up a Regency. However, it was not until January 11 that the Greek Civil War ended with a truce.

The battle line in Italy continued to inch forward, Forli on the Rimini-Bologna highway falling into Allied hands on November 9; Faenza, an important Italian city on the same highway, capitulating on December 17 to New Zealand troops of the Eighth Army. But the situation remained virtually static throughout January and February when the Allies were still inching their way toward Bologna.

THE ADVANCE ON JAPAN

GENERAL Douglas MacArthur's campaign of island hopping in the Pacific continued throughout the fall and winter, accompanied by paralyzing blows to Japanese sea and air power. In September alone the Yanks invaded Morotai Island near Halmahera, and Peleliu and Angaur in the Palaus group.

The war returned to the Philippines on October 20 when MacArthur's men invaded Leyte, securing the town of Tacloban with small casualties. Further inland opposition increased, however, and when the campaign ended on Christmas Day the Japanese had suffered 113,231 casualties, the United States 11,217.

The American assault on the Philippines goaded the Japanese Imperial Fleet into action. First sighted on October 21, the Japanese Navy sought to converge on Leyte Gulf in two forces from the Sibuyan and Sulu Seas, and

to strike with another force from the north. Admiral William F. Halsey's Third Fleet and Vice Admiral Thomas C. Kinkaid's Seventh Fleet engaged the enemy in a six day running battle, bombing, shelling, strafing, and torpedoing him mercilessly. Fifty-eight Japanese warships were sunk or damaged, including four carriers and two battleships sunk. This Second Battle of the Philippine Sea was a crucial defeat for the enemy's already depleted fleet.

On November 24 the Japanese homeland felt America's growing might when B-29 Superfortresses carried out a daylight raid on Tokyo for the first time since April, 1942. New attacks on the Japanese capital were made in succeeding weeks.

Island hopping continued on December 15 with the invasion of Mindoro, 155 miles south of Manila, without the loss of a single man. But the dramatic climax of the campaign was reached on the dawn of January 21 when General MacArthur returned to Luzon with a convoy of over 800 ships, going ashore at Lingayen Gulf against light resistance. Quickly consolidating an extensive beachhead, the Yanks poured inland and headed south for Manila. They overran the big air base at Clark Field on January 25 and on February 6 liberated most of Manila, freeing 5,000 prisoners of war and civilian internees.

In mid-February a new kind of attack was launched against Tokyo when 1,200 planes from an American task force near the Japanese mainland struck in a long-planned full-scale offensive. Two days later American marines invaded Iwo, a small inland only 750 miles from Tokyo. The fighting was as bloody as any in the war, but the marines were making progress and the end of the month found Japan's position precarious.

THE C.B.I. THEATER

AS MacArthur pressed his campaign in the Pacific, the Japanese were pursuing their conquest of China. They made headway throughout the fall, forcing the American 14th Air Force to abandon its air fields at Kweilin and Tanchuk in September and to destroy its Liuchow and Ishan bases in November. But on the other side of the ledger the British took Indaw in Burma and in January the Chinese captured Muse, joining another Chinese force that overcame Wanting. These successes eventuated in the reopening on January 22 of the Ledo-Burma Road from India to China. The important supply artery was renamed the Stilwell Road in honor of that American General.

THEIR FORCES ROUT NAZIS FROM FRANCE. As the sixth year of the war opened, Allied armies were sweeping through France to the very borders of the Reich. Among the geniuses of the great Allied offensive were, left to right, Lieut. Gen. George S. Patton, Commander of the U.S. Third Army; Lieut. General Omar N. Bradley, U.S. Twelfth Army Group Commander; and General Sir Bernard L. Montgomery, British Ground Forces Commander. Their forces sliced through northern France.

THE YANKS ENTER BELGIUM. Sweeping through France at the rate of more than 200 miles in four days, doughboys entered Belgium and Luxembourg and were warmly welcomed by the people of these small liberated countries. Even the children lavished flowers upon the conquering heroes, above, but freedom had its price and, in the picture at the left, a Belgian woman places flowers upon the body of an American soldier who was killed by German snipers in her backyard.

THE BRITISH REACH ANTWERP. By its lightning dash to Antwerp, the British Second Army cut off the entire Pas-de-Calais area, containing 100,000 Germans and many sites of the flying bombs. A long line of Nazi prisoners is shown in Antwerp and, below, Yanks inspect an underground flying bomb factory in the Metz area. Other bomb sites continued to launch their deadly cargoes for many weeks.

THE END OF THE ROAD. As the Allied Armies liberated France, the Maquis were quick to bring to justice those who had collaborated with the Nazis. Six young militiamen pleaded innocent at the Grenoble treason trial on September 2, but the court ruled them guilty of carrying arms against France. Shown as he faced the firing squad, this young man paid with his life while a large and eager crowd looked on

INFANTRY AND ARMOR PURSUE NAZIS. Yanks of an infantry division advance over a catwalk, above, as enemy shells burst wide of this bridge spanning the Meuse River near Houx, Belgium. In the picture below, American engineers hastily throw together a bridge at Namur, Belgium, for armored columns to follow the infantry in the drive across the Meuse River.

WITH THE 92ND DIVISION. A patrol of the all-Negro 92nd Division, above, blasts at a Nazi machine gun nest with a bazooka at an advanced position of the Fifth Army front in Italy. Soldiers of the same division guard a Nazi prisoner, sitting in the jeep. The Nazi was caught lurking behind the lines in civilian clothes, The captive waits sulkily to be transferred to a prison pen.

GIVES WILD WELCOME TO TROOPS. The tremendous ovation given British and Belgian soldiers entering Brussels was unlike anything hitherto seen in the War. Great scenes took place as the people wildly expressed their joy. The procession shown here was typical.

Justice catches up with Italian Fascists

TWO WAYS TO DIE. The wrath of the Italian people caught up with two Nazi collaborators during the first Fascist trials in Rome. Pietro Caruso, Fascist Police Chief of Rome, was tried and duly executed, but his assistant, Donato Carretta, was lynched by a mob of 7,000 who stormed the Palace of Justice Courtroom.

They got their hands on the luckless Carretta, dragged him into the street, beat and kicked him and threw him into the Tiber River. There he was thrust under water and drowned. Caruso, however, was saved from the mob, only to be tried, found guilty, and executed before a firing squad.

SHOT DOWN IN RETREAT. As the Germans retreated pell mell through Belgium they paid a heavy toll in casualties. These Nazis were caught in the open by Allied machine gunners near Mons, Belgium. American soldiers attend their wounds while a Belgian woman stands by helplessly. The lightning thrust from France through Belgium left the houses of this street standing intact.

ARTILLERY MAULS RETREATING NAZIS. The Allies shelled, bombed, and strafed the Nazi columns as they withdrew from France. An Allied armored column overtakes a shattered German column which was caught by Allied artillery-fire near Nancy. Below, two G.I.s pass through wreckage of an ammunition dump destroyed by retreating Nazis near Metz.

Fort Dinant falls to the Allies

NAZIS FLEE ACROSS THE MEUSE. Wrecking this bridge behind them, the Germans fled across the Meuse River as the U.S. First Army drove them back to the Reich where they were to make a strong stand for weeks. But at Dinant, Belgium, neither this destroyed bridge nor the fort could stop the Yanks.

TWO KINDS OF WELCOME. As the Allies rolled into Liege, Belgium, they were harassed by Nazi snipers, above, but the Belgian populace welcomed their liberators warmly, below. The tank in the picture above is firing at German snipers while the infantry hug the buildings for cover. Note the small Belgian lad standing against the building at the right.

THEY WERE THERE. Close on the heels of the doughboys on the Western Front were members of the W.A.C. (Women's Army Corps). Here they unload their own barrack bags in a rear area of a fighting zone in France. These soldiers operated their own convoy direct from England. The W.A.C. performed high service in support of the Yanks in the battle theaters of every front.

NAZI SYMPATHIZERS ARE ROUNDED UP. Following the entry of the American Seventh Army into Lyon on September 5, the French Forces of the Interior lost no time in rounding up collaborators. Some of the women have already had their hair clipped (the treatment accorded traitors) and are without shoes or stockings. Below, French troops and civilian duck machine gun bullets of Nazi sympathizers.

A STUBBORN TARGET. The great port and U-boat base of Brest was besieged for forty-six days before the Nazi defenders finally capitulated to American troops on September 21. The port was attacked not only by land but by air and here we see bombs of U.S. Army Eighth Air Force planes crashing on a gun emplacement and small quay of the Brest peninsula, in the northwestern part of France.

The Navy's big guns growl at a Jap convoy

ENTIRE CONVOY IS SUNK. A heavy cruiser takes pot shots at a Japanese convoy of thirty-two coastal cargo ships just off Mindanao in the Philippines. Two of the ships are trailing smoke off to the right of the picture and another vessel is getting the works. The entire thirty-two vessels as well as twenty sampans were sent to the bottom by Pacific Fleet carrier and surface forces commanded by Admiral William F. Halsey. This was the fleet's first attack against Mindanao and the total score of the action amounted to eighty-nine Japanese vessels of various categories, sunk or damaged, not including combat ships, and the destruction of sixty-eight enemy planes. In addition, five air fields and three ports were raked with destruction from the air. The damage to the Japanese merchant fleet was the most considerable of the war and was accomplished at no cost to our surface fleet and with only very light losses to our aircraft.

ON TO GERMANY. After the Allied armies had chased the Nazis out of France they swung the Maginot guns (top) around against the retreating Germans and assaulted the famed Siegfried Line, below. Yanks and their bulldozer tank pass easily through this break in the Westwall near Roetgen, Germany, but elsewhere resistance hardened and it took months to break through the defenses.

The remains of Le Havre

REDUCED TO RUBBLE. The Nazis gave up in the French seaport of Le Havre on September 12, but the once proud city of 200,000 inhabitants was a shambles. The Germans held out stubbornly long after the Allies had broken out of the Normandy pocket, and even as they capitulated to British forces, other Allied forces were at the German frontier. The determined defense of the channel ports by the Germans made it necessary for the Allies to divert thousands of troops to mopping up operations. Brest did not fall until September 21; the Nazis held a grip on the approaches to Antwerp until the British invaded Walcheren Island in November.

French girls welcome troops to Dijon

FLOWERS FOR LIBERATORS.
As liberating forces of the French First Army entered Dijon, young girls showered them with flowers. General Patch's Seventh Army drove up from Southern France and converged with General Patton's Third Army twelve and one half miles west of Dijon on September 12. This gave the Allies a continuous line along the French border. At the same time the British Second Army had pursued the enemy across northern France and into the Netherlands, while the Canadian First Army mopped up channel ports. The United States First Army was assaulting the Siegfried Line from Eupen to Trier in Germany.

LEADERS HOLD WAR TALKS.
A series of discussions concerning the conduct of the war against Germany and Japan was held at Quebec beginning on September 10 and continuing for a week. President Roosevelt and Prime Minister Churchill are shown in the top photograph and, below, Canada's Premier, Mr. Mackenzie King, is shown with Churchill. Marshal Stalin was also invited but was unable to leave the Soviet Union at that time. The Combined Chiefs of Staff were present for the Conference which ended on September 17 when a joint statement said that "all aspects of the war against Germany and Japan" had been discussed.

TRAGEDY IN LIEGE. Although the Nazis were driven from Liege, Belgium, on September 8, they struck back at the city by air, causing damage and casualties. Members of the United States First Army help to remove this Belgian boy from the ruins of a street following a raid by the Germans. Belgian civilians and volunteer war workers stand by tensely, horrified by the wantonness of war.

JAP BASE IS PUMMELLED. The systematic destruction of Japanese sea and air power continued in September. Carrier planes of the Pacific Fleet lashed the Nipponese positions on Cebu, Negros and Panay in the Central Philippines on Septembr 13, destroying 200 planes and sinking several ships. Cebu Harbor is shown here with its naval installations, warehouses and ships, billowing smoke.

NAZI HUNT. Red infantrymen scramble over a pile of wreckage in their hunt for Nazis in Praga, suburb of Warsaw. The Russians laid siege to Warsaw in July but bloody fighting resulted in a virtual stalemate until January 17 when the stubborn German resistance broke before the great Soviet winter offensive. For six months, however, the battle for Warsaw was deadlocked. Colonel-General Batov, Hero of the Soviet Union, studying map, right, commanded the armies fighting on Warsaw's outskirts. When the breakthrough finally came, Warsaw was in ruins.

Raiding supply lines in Italy

LEGNANO ARTERY SEVERED. As the American Fifth and British Eighth Armies hurled themselves upon the Gothic Line below Bologna, planes blasted at the life lines of the Germans in the areas to the north. Here a Martin B-26 Marauder of the Tactical Air Force scores a direct hit on the center of the road bridge at Legnano and also hits both rail bridges. On September 21 the Eighth Army succeeded in pushing the Nazis out of Rimini and two days later the Fifth Army had a firm grip on Futa Pass. The drive was short-lived, however, and for many months the Nazis clung to their positions with bloody fanaticism. Mud, rain, and biting temperatures further hampered the Allied advance, but they continued to hack their way by inches toward Bologna.

The marines storm Peleliu

PALAU GROUP IS INVADED.
Landings on the islands belonging to the Palau group, 300 miles from the Philippines, began on September 14 when the marines swarmed on Peleliu under a heavy curtain of naval and air bombardment. When this picture was taken on D-day, not a marine had yet landed and the whole island was ablaze as the leathernecks of the First Division streaked towards the hostile beaches. Upon reaching the beaches the marines were met by determined ground forces and fierce artillery and mortar fire but they nevertheless pushed ahead rapidly. In the following days other landings were made on Angaur by army troops of the Eighty-first (Wildcat) Infantry Division and troops also went ashore at Morotai. General MacArthur accompanied his men in the latter operation and had this to say to his troops: "You have done well. You now dominate the last stronghold which barred you from the Philippines. The enemy, as usual, was not in the right places at the right time."

UNDER FIRE. The first wave of marines to hit the sands of Peleliu was greeted with scathing mortar fire. Amphibious tractors, which were knocked out by direct hits as they brought in the assault troops, still burn in the background, and the leathernecks keep low to avoid the deadly mortar shells. Other troops are still being landed in the far distance, lower picture.

IMPORTANT LAND BASE IS LIBERATED. On September 14 Chinese troops advancing from Yunnan into North Burma took the important city of Tengchung. This was the first big Chinese city to be recaptured after eight years of war, and as a strong Japanese base it had been the main obstacle to linking together the Burma and Ledo roads. The battle lasted five weeks and 3,000 Japanese died in the fighting. Top picture: Chinese in Tengchung again; bottom: Chinese gunners in hills above Tengchung.

SNIPER'S VICTIM. Opposition was heavier on Peleliu than on either Angaur or Morotai. Here, a member of a marine demolition squad is evacuated after being hit by a sniper's bullet. The steel helmet, which he still clutches, plainly shows the bullet hole. He and his buddies were assigned to blast the Japs from their hideouts in the crannies and caves of the island's jungle lairs.

ANOTHER ISLAND FALLS. The small island of Morotai fell quickly under the combined blows of the Army, Navy and Air Forces. American assault troops and heavy armor are shown crowding the enemy into the interior of Morotai.

MOVE TO FLANK SIEGFRIED LINE. British Horsa and Hamilcar gliders land on Dutch soil. They were part of the First Allied Airborne Army which invaded Holland September 17 in a daring bid to turn the northern tip of the Siegfried Line. The Army was unloaded from more than 1,000 air transports and gliders in the region of Arnhem and Nijmegen. After a heroic nine-day stand, the skytroops withdrew.

Opening the battle for Germany

September, 1944

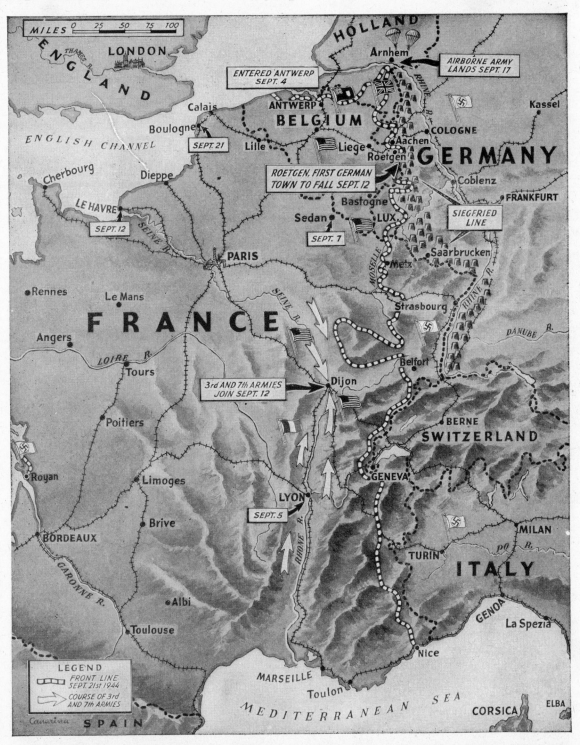

A NEW PHASE BEGINS. With the speedy drive through France to the borders of the Reich, the battle of France had ended and the battle for Germany was begun. In many places the Siegfried Line had been reached and the Allies made a quick and daring bid to turn the northern end of the line with airborne troops. This was unsuccessful and many weeks were consumed in breaking the Westwall defenses.

TOSS STEEL AT THE NAZIS. Quickly setting up a six-pound anti-tank gun, skytroops in the Arnhem pocket fire at a German self-propelled gun a short distance away and, in the lower picture, a three-inch mortar is used against enemy positions. The British Second Army, driving from Eindhoven, was able to reach Nijmegen and capture a vital bridge, but Airborne troops at Arnhem were forced to withdraw.

Hollanders welcome the British

EINDHOVEN IS LIBERATED. When the British Second Army, together with airborne troops, captured Eindhoven, they received a tumultuous welcome by the Dutch populace. Flags and bunting were hung in the streets and crowds cheered as the heavy armor rolled by. Below, a group of Dutch nurses waves greetings. The British troops pushed on to Nijmegen but were unable to save trapped sky troops at Arnhem.

The British capture Nijmegen bridge September 22, 1944

THE WAAL RIVER IS CROSSED. In their race to relieve surrounded airborne troops at Arnhem, the British Second Army seized the vital Nijmegen bridge across the Waal River after fierce fighting. An Allied tank passes two dead Nazis, above, and the picture below indicates further the bitterness of the battle. Despite this success, the encircled troops could not be reached.

SKYWAY FEEDS BELEAGUERED TROOPS. A supply basket floats down by parachute to First Allied Airborne troops in Holland. The troops were cut off at Arnhem and less than 2,000 of the original 8,000 were able to withdraw across the Lower Rhine. But the battle had cost the Nazis 12,000 to 15,000 dead and gave the Allies time to broaden their corridor through Holland.

HE ESCAPED. Major General R. Urquhart, D.S.O., was the General commanding the First Airborne Division at Arnhem. The 42-year-old General was captured by the enemy but escaped and was among the 2,000 who came back across the River Lek. The picture shows him at his headquarters in the last British stronghold in the Arnhem pocket. He stands beside the airborne flag.

ELUDE NAZI CAPTORS. British paratroopers make good their escape across the Rhine after being captured by Germans in the last outpost on Arnhem bridge. They had been taken to Germany but escaped through a German town and a woods. They found the rowboat in which they are shown landing at Nijmegen. Here they joined the British Second Army. All but 2,000 of 8,000 troops were wiped out.

NAZIS LEAVE THEIR MARK. Tallinn, capital of Estonia, was liberated by the Soviets on September 22, but the Nazis left in their wake such atrocities as the funeral pyre, below, which was found at Klooga, southwest of Tallinn. Soviet prisoners were forced to build wood piles like the one shown, after which they were shot and burned. The Nazis left too hastily to burn these victims.

TOUGH GOING. United States Army trucks, manned by Negro troops, negotiate a difficult by-pass through mountains southwest of Bologna. The American Fifth and the British Eighth Armies put a dent in the Nazi Gothic Line in September, taking Pistoia, Rimini, and Futa Pass, but they were unable to exploit the rupture and remained stalled in severe fighting below Bologna for months.

ANOTHER FRONT IS OPENED. A Russian gun pounds a German frontier position in preparation for a drive across the Czechoslovakian border on September 24. In the picture below, an angry-faced Red infantryman holds the head of a fallen comrade while other infantrymen bend low and charge across a railway track in the battle for a Nazi-held depot in the Carpathian foothills.

ROUGHING IT. Although this nurse, attached to a field hospital in Luxembourg, must take her bath from a helmet, she can grin at discomfort. American nurses moved right along with the armies and while they worked long and hard hours caring for the wounded, it was often necessary for them to share also the discomforts and inconveniences of battle conditions.

BETWEEN BATTLES. Two Yanks wave a greeting and call "Hiya, Toots" to a scantily clad window dummy that has been bombed out of its window in Merkstein, Germany. And below, four American infantrymen relax in the library of Rimberg Castle on the Dutch-German frontier. One G.I. reaches for a book while the others help themselves to preserves—but they keeps their guns handy.

The British begin the liberation of Greece

ΣΥΝΟΙΚΙΑ
ΑΝΘΕΙΑ

WELCOMED BY POPULACE. British amphibious forces invaded Greece at Katakolon on September 26 following landings from the air two days earlier. Little opposition was met and by October 4 Patras, third largest city in Greece, was liberated. The impoverished citizenry of Patras, above, warmly welcomed the troops, and a few days later Corinth, below, was also liberated.

Supplies move up in Italy

TRANSPORT PROBLEM. Fighting in the mountainous country of the Apennines, where many stone-built villages favored the defenders, proved a severe test for the Allied supply and transportation organization. In many places the terrain was so difficult that laden mules were used to carry supplies for the infantry. Many remarkable feats of bridge-building were achieved by Allied engineers, upon whose work the speed of the advance largely depended. Picture on the left shows a Bailey bridge thrown across a 530-foot gap on the Fifth Army front. Above, Eighth Army vehicles wind over the hills.

Bombs and leaflets fall on Burma

HEAVY AIR ATTACKS IN BURMA. During October many powerful blows were struck against important Japanese communications and supply routes in Burma in support of the advancing Fourteenth Army by the Strategic Air Force of Eastern Air Command. The picture above shows a direct hit from an R.A.F. Liberator bursting on enemy railway yards at Ye, near the main line running from Bangkok to Rangoon. Right, propaganda leaflets shower from an attacking plane after a heavy raid on an enemy rail station.

WOMEN AND CHILDREN SEEK SAFETY. As British troops of Lieutenant General Sir Miles Dempsey's Second Army fought the Nazis in and about Hertogenbosch, the lives of Dutch civilians were imperiled. In the picture above, a Dutch civilian frantically rushes two small children off the street to safety and, below, a family takes refuge in a dugout while Tommies engage the enemy.

STRIKE RYUKYU CHAIN. Planes from fast carriers of Admiral Nimitz's Pacific Fleet hit targets in the industrial area of Naha City on Okinawa Island in the Ryukyu chain south of Japan. These vast plumes of smoke stem from stricken ships and warehouses, at least four ships having been fired.

ROYAL TOUR. In October Britain's King George flew across the channel to make a five-day tour of the battlefields of France, Belgium and Holland and visit the Allied forces in the front line. In the course of this tour he motored more than 200 miles in a single day in order to confer the K.B.C. on Lieut. Gen. Omar Bradley, Commander of the Twelfth Army Group. The King travelled about usually in a jeep and slept each night in an army caravan as the guest of Field Marshal Montgomery. He received a warm welcome not only from the fighting men but also from crowds of civilians in the liberated towns and villages through which he passed. The picture shows the King, left, enjoying a joke with General Dwight D. Eisenhower, center, while General Bradley (left, rear) and General Courtney Hodges stand by.

TWO-WAY TRAVEL. The National Liberation Army of Yugoslavia triumphantly enters Belgrade, capital of Yugoslavia, which it helped liberate with the Soviet forces in October. In the picture below, German war gear litters a road over which the Nazis hastily fled from the city. Yugoslavian peasant women walk along the battle-scarred highway and a man searches the rubble for valuables.

Air and sea forces liberate Athens

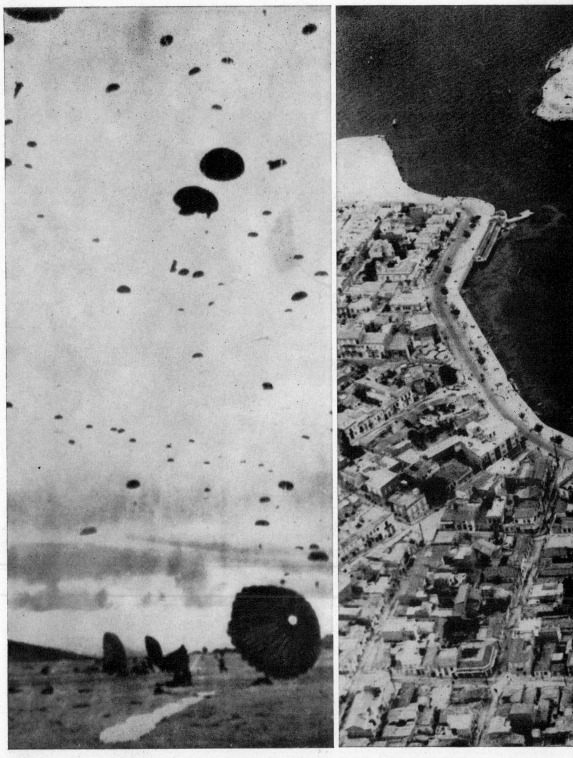

GREEK CAPITAL IS FREED. British troops occupied Greece against only light resistance, most of the German forces being withdrawn to prevent being cut off by the Russians and the Yugoslav partisans. British paratroopers dropped near Athens, left, from C-47s of the United States 12th Air Force troop car-

rier command, and naval forces moved into the great Athens port of Piraeus. The British were aided by Greek patriots who forgot factional differences long enough to oust the Nazi tyrants. But for the most part the Germans fled without a fight.

Athens celebrates its freedom

THE NAZIS ARE GONE. After three and one half years under the Nazi yoke, citizens of Athens celebrated their liberation with a Victory Parade, in which they carried British and American flags. However, the Nazi tyranny had left many cruel dislocations and the undernourished had to be fed at soup kitchens such as the one below, where a long queue waits for a ration of uncooked dried beans and soup powder.

FALLS TO YANKS. After more than one week of fierce street battles, the German city of Aachen fell to the American First Army on October 20. Ten days earlier the Americans had presented a "surrender or die" ultimatum to the German garrison, but as no reply was received the attack on the city was resumed. Here, United States envoys carry surrender ultimatum to the Germans.

ONLY A SHELL IS LEFT. The German town of Aachen, formerly with a population of 165,000, was completely pulverized by Allied dive bombers and artillery before the main Nazi defenders withdrew, leaving only a small garrison to resist. Many civilians picked their way through the battle lines to safety rather than submit to the pounding given the SS garrison.

BAGGED AT AACHEN. American G.I.s had heard much about the officer caste in the German Army. Here a doughboy gets a close-up of a group of Nazi officers nabbed in Aachen when that city fell to the Allies. Not only these swaggering Nazi youths were inconvenienced by the battling around Aachen, but also the civilians, below, who are evacuating their homes near Aachen.

A mighty armada returns to the Philippines

DAWN ATTACK ON LEYTE. When the Americans were forced out of the Philippines General Douglas MacArthur had said, "I shall return." Exactly two years and six months later he did. At dawn on October 20 large naval forces approached the eastern coast of Leyte Island in the central Philippines, just 300 miles north of Morotai. The fleet is shown here just before the major amphibious operation was launched. At one stroke the Japanese in the Philippines were split into two forces. Landings were quickly effected under cover of a violent naval and air barrage. The troops and heavy armor pushed inland against light resistance and rapidly gained control of the coastal road and seized the town of Tacloban. But the campaign lasted two months before the Japanese were finally defeated on Leyte. The price: 11,217 American casualties as against 113,231 Japanese casualties.

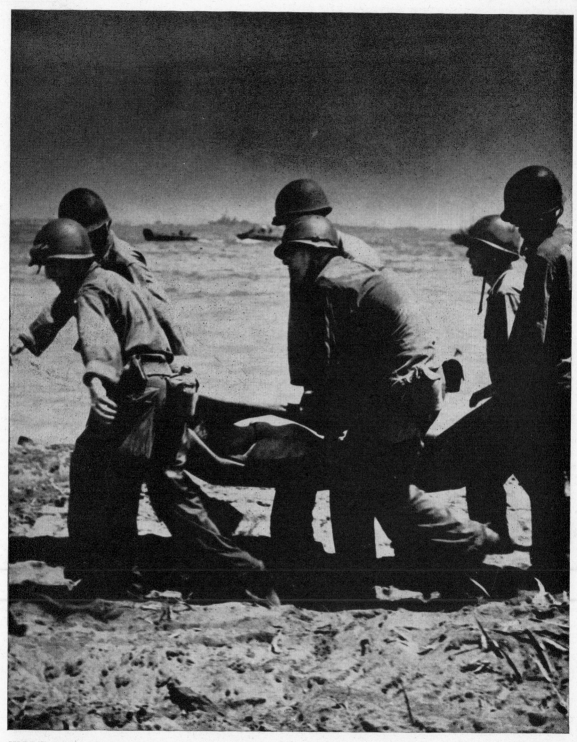

WAR'S GRIM PRICE. A victim of the initial assault on Leyte, an American casualty is carried in a makeshift litter by his buddies. He was caught in the fierce Japanese fire that swept the beach during the first landings, and landing craft may still be seen speeding shoreward from units of the task force in the background. One litter-bearer looks fearfully inland.

PURSUE FOE INLAND. After earlier assault waves had secured the beachhead these huge, heavily armored "alligators" ground up the beach for the drive inland. They added great power to the infantry forces battling the enemy in the interior. Large LSTs, their jaws gaping open, are in the background, as well as the Coast Guard and Naval personnel who manned them.

The Nazis crush Polish patriots

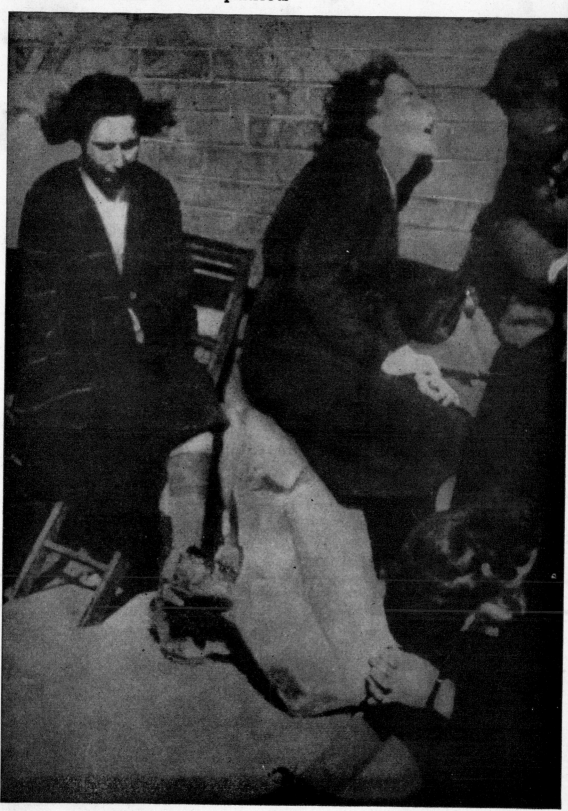

WARSAW TRAGEDY. On October 21 the heroic defenders of Warsaw fired their last shots in the struggle to seize the city from the German troops in occupation. For over two months the Polish Patriot Army had waged a gallant fight, but the exhaustion of all weapons and food supplies compelled them to cease resistance. Hope of relief from outside vanished when attempts by the Red Army, with Polish formations, to cross the Vistula failed. The pictures here show: left, some of the starving civilians of Warsaw after the rising; above, Germans blindfold Polish delegates to discuss the terms of surrender; right, a party of Polish patriots being marched away after the capitulation of the city was signed.

The Jap fleet comes out for a whipping

BOMBS SHAKE THE YAMATO. When the Yanks invaded Leyte, two large Japanese naval forces steamed into the central Philippines with the intention of disrupting the American supply lines and harassing the landings. But Vice Admiral Thomas C. Kinkaid's Seventh Fleet smashed the attempt, sinking or damaging every ship in the southern enemy force. Further north other units of the Japanese Imperial Fleet were intercepted by Admiral William F. Halsey's Third Fleet and decisively defeated and routed. Elements of the Third Fleet also assisted in the action in the central Philippines and it was from the Third Fleet that the Yamato was fleeing when she was attacked by a Curtiss Helldiver. The great battlewagon is pictured here as it shuddered under two direct bomb hits. In the complete action of the Second Battle of the Philippine Sea the Nipponese Navy was so devastatingly defeated that it could no longer offer serious resistance to the advancing American forces in the Pacific. Japan's total losses in this battle were 58 warships sunk or damaged, including four carriers and two battleships. American losses were negligible.

American carriers run into trouble

THE PRINCETON GOES DOWN. Among the Pacific Fleet's losses was the light carrier U. S. S. Princeton shown billowing smoke, right, after its magazine was hit by Japanese bombs. Directly next to the ill-fated carrier is a cruiser, standing by to aid in the rescue of the Princeton's crew. In the picture at the left, the

crew of one escort carrier rushes to launch fighters as the CVE in the background zigzags a perilous path through salvos from a Japanese cruiser. The United States lost, in addition to the Princeton, two escort carriers, two destroyers, and one destroyer escort.

PT CREWS IN THE THICK OF IT. The crews of PT boats played an important part in the Second Battle of the Philippine Sea, not only in spotting and attacking Jap naval forces, but also in rescue work. They saved great numbers of our own personnel and also picked up many Japanese survivors. But they are taking no chances—they rescue these Japs at gun point.

The Second Battle of the Philippine Sea October, 1944

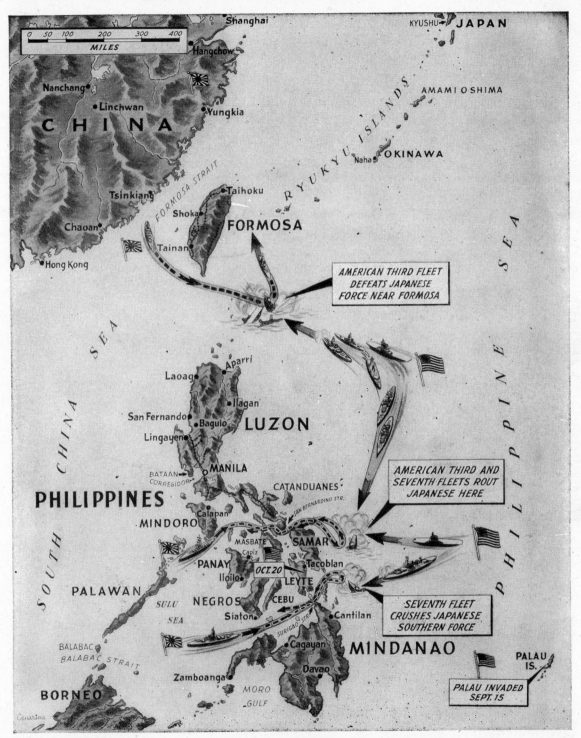

NAVAL DISASTER FOR THE JAPS. When American forces invaded the Philippines, the Japanese Imperial Fleet came out in strength to challenge the United States Pacific Fleet. The results for the Japs were catastrophic. The Third and Seventh Fleets took up the challenge in the central Philippines and in the Formosa area and decisively defeated and put to rout the major part of the Nipponese Navy.

SUCCESSES IN BURMA. During October British and Indian troops of the Fourteenth Army made good progress in Burma after months of heavy fighting for the important Tiddim Road amid difficult conditions. Tiddim itself, prewar center of the Chin Hills territory, was captured on October 19. Above, Royal Scots Fusiliers seek out enemy snipers in a Burmese village and, below, other Fusiliers cross a swirling stream in the jungle with their rifles, spades and bagpipes. One Scot debonairly plays his bagpipe.

Honors for heroes of sea battle

MEN AND OFFICERS ARE DECORATED. In the picture above, Admiral William F. Halsey, commander of the Navy's Third Fleet, reads a citation awarding the Navy Cross to Rear Admiral R. B. Carney, left, his chief of staff, for services rendered during the Second Battle of the Philippine Sea. Standing at Admiral Halsey's shoulder is his aide, Commander Harold E. Stassen, former Governor of Minnesota, holding the medal. In the picture at the right, Rear Admiral W. L. Ainsworth, commander of cruisers and destroyers, Pacific Fleet, awards the Purple Heart to wounded veterans of the Pacific Fleet's action in the Philippines.

The Nazis launch the rocket bomb

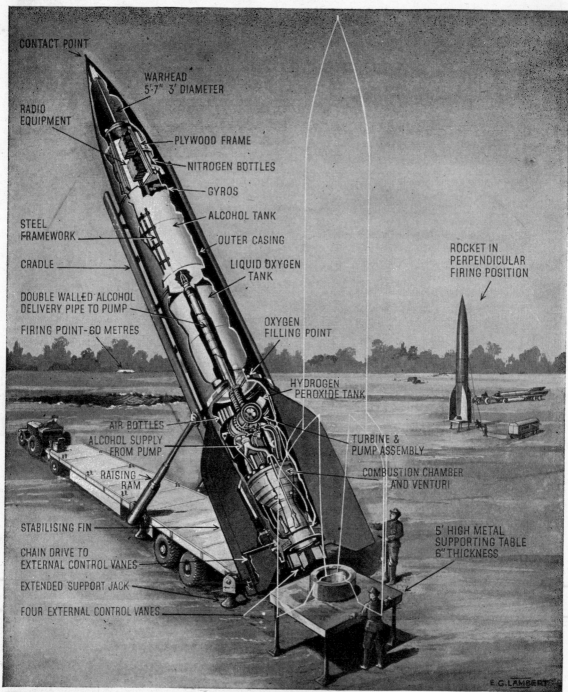

CONTACT POINT

WARHEAD
5·7" 3' DIAMETER

RADIO
EQUIPMENT

PLYWOOD FRAME

NITROGEN BOTTLES

GYROS

ALCOHOL TANK

STEEL
FRAMEWORK

OUTER CASING

CRADLE

LIQUID OXYGEN
TANK

DOUBLE WALLED ALCOHOL
DELIVERY PIPE TO PUMP

FIRING POINT-60 METRES

OXYGEN
FILLING POINT

ROCKET IN
PERPENDICULAR
FIRING POSITION

HYDROGEN
PEROXIDE TANK

AIR BOTTLES
ALCOHOL SUPPLY
FROM PUMP

TURBINE &
PUMP ASSEMBLY

RAISING
RAM

COMBUSTION CHAMBER
AND VENTURI

STABILISING FIN

CHAIN DRIVE TO
EXTERNAL CONTROL VANES

5' HIGH METAL
SUPPORTING TABLE
6" THICKNESS

EXTENDED SUPPORT JACK

FOUR EXTERNAL CONTROL VANES

E.G.LAMBERT

GERMAN ROCKET-BOMB. Early in October the enemy began in earnest their rocket-bomb attacks against southern England, and these continued through the autumn and winter months. While the rocket was much less accurate than the flying-bomb, it was a more deadly weapon, making a crater 30 ft. deep and causing damage over a wide area. Much larger than the flying-bomb, its warhead contained 2,000 lb. of explosive. Its flight could not be intercepted and, moreover, the small platforms used as launching sites were hard to destroy by bombing. Most of the rockets which fell in England were fired from sites in Holland. The weapon had a range of about 200 miles and ascended 60 or 70 miles during flight. This special drawing illustrates detailed construction of the rocket-bomb, and shows how it is raised into firing position. Right, rescue work after rocket incident in London.

WITH THE 92ND DIVISION. Members of the all-Negro 92nd Division pour a stream of fire on the Nazi Gothic Line in Italy. This was as tough a front as any in the war and the men are glad to stand in line, below, to get a welcome shower to wash away the dirt and grime of many days of active combat duty in a rough sector.

Mosquitoes sting the Gestapo October 31, 1944

GERMAN HEADQUARTERS IS BOMBED. On October 31 a daring low-level attack was made by Mosquitoes of the R.A.F. Tactical Air Force on the Gestapo headquarters housed in the University of Aarhus, Denmark. Two adjoining four-story buildings formed the target, and to obtain accuracy in bombing a model was especially built for the crews. The top photograph shows two of the Mosquitoes over the target with bombs falling; the picture below, taken by a reconnaissance plane from almost roof-top height, shows the success of the attack.

British and Canadians invade Walcheren

STORM DUTCH ISLAND. On November 1 British Commandos and British and Canadian infantry landed at Flushing and Westkapelle on the island of Walcheren. This operation was launched in order to clear the enemy from the approaches to the port of Antwerp, the use of which was vital to the Allied armies fighting on the Western front. The Flushing force crossed the Scheldt estuary in assault craft, and although enemy fire from shore defences was less fierce than anticipated, many submerged obstacles caused the loss of some landing-craft. After very stiff fighting ashore British and Canadian troops had cleared most of Flushing by nightfall. Although the Royal Marine Commandos met deadly opposition at Westkapelle, and many landing-craft were sunk, they charged ashore through a gap in the dyke, captured three of the biggest enemy batteries, and soon established a firm bridgehead. Pictures show: left, tank landing craft approaching beach at Westkapelle: bottom left, British Commandos advancing along waterfront at Flushing with shells bursting ahead; bottom right, evacuating wounded at Flushing.

CASUALTIES MARK CIVIL STRIFE. As Athens police and demonstrators fire on one another, both sides fling themselves on the ground to avoid being hit. In the picture below, a left wing demonstrator lies sprawled in a gutter. The Greek Civil War did not end until January 11 when a truce was signed after Britain's Prime Minister Winston Churchill had intervened.

SUCCESSOR TO GENERAL LEESE. Lieutenant General Sir Richard McCreery, center, is shown leaving Greek headquarters on the Italian Front with Colonel Tasklaotos, right, and other aides, after a visit to a Greek brigade north of Rimini. General McCreery succeeded Sir Oliver Leese as commander of the British Eighth Army in Italy. General Leese, former commander, took a post in southeast Asia.

ON THE RECEIVING END OF ALLIED FIRE. This captured German photograph shows SS Grenadiers seeking shelter from American heavy artillery behind a high stone wall. Under attack on their own frontier, these Nazis appear sullen and unhappy as they wait out a violent Allied artillery barrage.

DUTCH CHILDREN ARE EVACUATED. As the war swept into the Netherlands, the lot of children was particularly hard. Thousands of them had to be uprooted from their homes and evacuated to areas of safety. The youngster above, with the improvised stockings and huge suitcase, is waiting for a lorry which will take him further from the terrors of battle. The little Dutch girl is clutching a bag of candy which was given her by an Allied soldier.

HOLLANDERS KNEEL IN GRIEF. Villagers of Leende, near Eindhoven, kneel and pray in the street for four victims who were killed by the retreating Nazis. In the picture below, another kind of victim is shown in a Nijmegen stocking factory which was converted into a refuge for the aged.

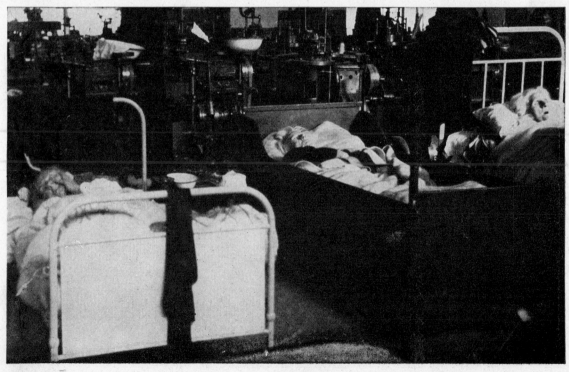

FAMILIES BECOME REFUGEES. As the war was carried into the Reich itself, it was now the turn of German civilians to experience something of what their Fuehrer had mercilessly inflicted upon millions of innocent people elsewhere in Europe. The pictures on this page show German families on the move as Allied progress overwhelms their towns and villages. At the top, a typical German housewife takes her belongings to safety; at the bottom, civilians leave a fighting area.

SUPPLIES ARE DROPPED. While the tremendous increase in American air power throughout the Far East took the war to the very heart of the Japanese homeland, it brought much-needed assistance and relief to the valiant native armies of China. Powerful air forces flew from distant bases in India and the liberated parts of Burma to drop ammunition, equipment and supplies to the Chinese.

KONZ-KARTHAUS BRIDGE IS HIT. Bombs from Marauders of the United States Army Ninth Air Force land flush on the Konz-Karthaus rail bridge over the Moselle River, five miles southwest of Trier. The rear areas of the Westwall were subjected to almost continual blasting by Allied planes in an effort to starve out the German forces manning the formidable Siegfried defense system.

ALLIES BLAST BRIDGES. While the Allies advanced in Burma and in the Pacific, Japanese troops continued their successes in China. However, the Allies put up desperate resistance, demolishing this bridge and railroad over the Li Shui riverbed just ten miles north of the threatened city of Kweilin which the Japs entered shortly afterward, pushing the 14th Air Force back to Kunming.

LAUNCH NEW OFFENSIVE. Despite heavy rains on the Third Army Front, General Patton launched an offensive on November 8, the first in nearly six weeks. The entire western front had been comparatively quiet for several weeks with only inconclusive fighting between the American First Army and German infantry in the Huertgen Forest disturbing the relative peacefulness of the battle zones.

FREE PARIS CELEBRATES. The Nazis are no longer in Paris after nearly five years of occupation, and the French commemorate Armistice Day with a parade and ceremonies at the tomb of the unknown soldier. England's Prime Minister Winston Churchill was present for the occasion as was France's General Charles de Gaulle, shown as they marched and rode together in the procession.

The pride of the German Navy is sunk November 12, 1944

R.A.F. BOMBS SINK THE TIRPITZ. The last big battleship of the German Navy was sunk on November 12 when twenty-nine Royal Air Force Lancasters dropped three six-ton "earthquake" bombs along the whole length of the mighty battle wagon. The once proud vessel, below, is shown in the picture above as she lay a useless hulk in the Tromso Fjord, Norway.

TERRAIN TROUBLE. Natural obstacles combined with Nazi destruction to harass the Russians in their drive to knock the Germans out of the Carpathian Mountains. A Soviet gun crew trains its rifle on an enemy strong point far down the valley, and in the other scene the Germans have made their pursuit even more difficult by blasting a railway into twisted wreckage. The Russians began their long campaign to clear the Germans out of the Carpathian Mountains in September.

ATTACK SUPPLY ROUTES. While the Allies were held to a virtual stalemate at the Gothic Line near Bologna, U. S. fliers from Italian bases ranged far and wide over Nazi targets in the rear. Here United States Army 12th Air Force medium bombers attack the Piacenza rail bridge in northern Italy. The valuable supply route becomes a puff of smoke under American bombs.

Carriers gut Jap shipping in Manila Harbor

NO PLACE TO HIDE. American carrier planes left this scene of destruction at Manila Harbor on November 19. The vessel in the foreground is scuttled, another is blazing furiously, while the one in the center

background is floundering from a near-hit. Smoke pours from blazing shore installations. During the raid 118 Japanese planes were also destroyed.

Patton's men fight their way into Metz

CLEAR STREETS OF GERMANS. As the Allied November offensive on the Western Front reached its crescendo, the American Third Army crashed into the streets of Metz. A tank destroyer with a 90-mm gun takes up a position overlooking Herman Goering Street and, below, a patrol of infantrymen picks its way gingerly through Metz in search of remaining Nazi snipers.

Yank artillery on wheels

PLENTY OF FIRE POWER HERE. A convoy of artillery, above, manned by a Negro unit, pauses while the outfit "takes a break." The multiple rocket launcher, below, is mounted on a tank and fires 4.5 inch rockets. The rockets are fired singly, the multiple effect here being a result of a time exposure photograph. The gun is pictured in action on the Seventh Army front in France.

Bridging the Belfort Gap

THE FRENCH ENTER BELFORT. Soldiers of the French First Army, commanded by General de Tassigny, moved through the vital Belfort Gap on November 20 and the American Seventh Army struck into the Vosges passes. The French made a sensational 30 mile advance in two days, reaching the Rhine near Switzerland. French patrols entered Mulhouse and the American Seventh Army took Sarrebourg in the rapid general advance at the southern end of the Western Front, but to the north, American and British forces were meeting stiff resistance. In this picture of a mine-blasted over-pass in Belfort, French soldiers are shown as they escorted an old woman through the debris.

CELEBRATE LIBERATION. Even before the Nazis were completely driven from Metz, these young people of the town raised their voices in song at the junction of the Hermann Goering-Strasse and Adolph Hitler-Strasse. In the picture below, two American soldiers of the Fifth Infantry Division examine the battered casemate of Fort Driant, one of the key defense forts of Metz.

THE NAZIS ARE CLEARED FROM A GERMAN TOWN. A French artillery unit of the American Seventh Army is shown as it shelled the Nazis out of the streets of Strasbourg. In the picture below, German prisoners are made to clear away the rubble and damage caused by the artillery barrage.

A RESCUE CREW GIVES AID. A badly injured airman, his unconscious form strapped to a special stretcher, is gently lowered from the wreckage of a building in southern England following the explosion of a German V-bomb. The Nazi horror weapon harassed southern England for months after France was liberated, but the English continued to "take it."

DOGS DETECT MINES. Engineers of the British Second Army employed dogs to help them spot mines on the Helmond-Venlo railway at the town of Amerika on the Western Front. The town was reached on November 23 and engineers immediately went to work to clear the railway for use. The dog in the foreground apparently has smelled out a hidden explosive. But while trained dogs helped to solve the mine problem, stray livestock that got in the battle lines created another problem. The two stray horses being brought in by a British soldier were placed in an enclosure behind the battle area. Animals were returned when properly claimed.

Superfortresses bomb Tokyo in daylight raid

A LARGE FORCE BLASTS INDUSTRY. The capital of Japan was subjected to an air attack for the first time since April 18, 1942, when a sizable force of B-29s, based in the Marianas, struck at the city's industry on November 24, 1944. The large picture at the right shows the city's most densely populated section as it looks from a Superfortress. At the bottom of the picture is the Sumida River and at the upper left is a drainage canal. The blockwide strips are wartime firebreaks. When our airmen bombed the Tokyo area they flew over the Japanese imperial palace grounds and took the picture above, but saved their bombs for industrial targets. The palace grounds, in the heart of Japan's congested capital, are encircled by a moat which is clearly visible in the picture.

ON THE BRITISH SECOND ARMY FRONT. In addition to road mines, the dispatch rider, above, must push his way through knee-deep mud and water. Dispatchers were a prime target, also, for snipers. A young Hollander gives th's messenger a helping hand. In the picture below, a tank crew under fire slogs through the mud to the protection of their armored "home."

CIVILIANS SUFFER. After the Germans retreated from France, they loosed their V-bombs against pursuing Allied troops and against Belgian and French towns. They were ineffective against military targets, but wrought horrible destruction upon civilians. The wounded and dead lie in a street in a Belgian town as a priest stands ready to administer last rites.

A miracle of supply at Leyte

THE OCEAN IS NO BARRIER. A bridge of ships formed a supply line to Leyte the moment the beaches were cleared. This armada of LSTs is shown pouring supplies ashore at a Tacloban airstrip.

EN ROUTE TO LEYTE. These members of the Women's Army Corps were the first to arrive in the Palau Islands in the Pacific. They stopped there en route to duty at Leyte in the Philippines. The girls above did not forget their mascot, a black kitten. The smiling miss at the left makes a striking picture, framed by the wreck of a Japanese plane on the Peleliu airstrip. The W.A.C. performed valuable non-combatant service with the troops in many overseas theaters, sharing the hardships and discomforts of the rear battle areas.

AS YOU SOW, YE ARE LIKE TO REAP. A glum-faced, grim Hitler, surrounded by downcast Nazi leaders, surveys the ravages of war in a town on the Western Front. This film was captured by the United States Army Signal Corps. In World War I Germany did not experience the devastation that both air attacks and ground assaults caused in the Second World War.

Engineering feat in Burma

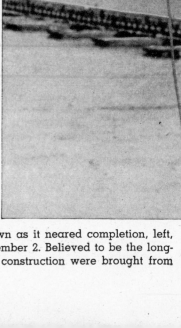

SPANNING THE CHINDWIN. This 1096 foot floating Bailey Bridge, shown as it neared completion, left, was built across the Chindwin River after the capture of Kalewa on December 2. Believed to be the longest bridge of its kind in any theater of war at the time, sections for its construction were brought from

Calcutta over 320 miles of winding mountain road. Bengal sappers and miners accomplished the job. Barrage balloons, the first to fly over Burma, protected the bridge. The Chindwin River was first crossed by 14th Army assault troops.

ENTER WITHOUT KNOCKING. Seventh Army infantrymen go after a German sniper in a house in Niederbronn, France. One Yank stands well back while he gingerly prepares to swing open a door. Two other G.I.'s hold their guns tensely ready to deal quickly and firmly with whatever happens after the door opens. After a town's fall, snipers and booby traps were always a menace to be eliminated.

CLEARING THE VOSGES MOUNTAINS. French troops played an important role in driving the Germans back through the passes in the Vosges mountains. Here, they are shown using mules to carry supplies over the mountainous terrain and, below, 155 millimeter howitzers roar at the enemy near Mulhouse, also on the southern front.

HE'LL TAKE A CHANCE. Ignoring the sign in this street of a Western Front town, a British tankman dashes toward a Nazi sniper nest. Another Tommy crouches on the sidewalk with revolver ready. In the picture below, British troops seek cover behind trees and a truck as they go after Nazi snipers in a bullet riddled street of Blerick, on the Western Front.

THE ENGINEERS FIND A WAY. Italy's many rivers helped to slow the Allied advance up the Italian boot. On the night of December 4, British troops attacked across the River Lamone, southwest of Faenza, and secured a beachhead. Following this victory, sappers immediately started construction on the trestle bridge, shown here, to allow armor and artillery to cross in support of the infantry.

MOBILE ARTILLERY POURS IT ON. A Yank self-propelled gun in the Ribeauville area of France, north of Mulhouse, fires on German positions in the Rhine valley. Haguenau, communications center leading into the Saar Basin from the southeast, fell to General Patch's Seventh Army on December 11 and gains were made along the entire Allied front.

GERMANY'S VOLKSSTURM PREPARES TO FIGHT. While the main task of the Home Guard in Britain was over, the swift advance of the Allied armies into the Reich made necessary the formation of a German "People's Army." In the middle of October, when Germany was already being invaded from the east and west, Hitler had delivered an emergency proclamation calling on all male Germans between sixteen and sixty, able to carry arms, to prepare themselves for the defense of the Fatherland. Volkssturm units were hastily formed in many towns and villages, each under the command of reliable Nazi party officials. Some were provided with uniforms, but most wore civilian clothes with an arm-band bearing the German emblem. Above, a Volkssturm parade in Berlin.

AN AID TO NIGHT ACTION. A powerful searchlight illuminates the terrain in a forward area of th
British Eighth Army on the Italian front. Searchlights of this type played an important role on this fron
creating a moonlihgt effect over roads, rivers, tracks and obstacles, to assist drivers moving supplies t
forward areas within a few thousand yards of enemy front line positions.

CAVALRY ATTACK IN EAST PRUSSIA. Soviet horsemen sweep across the fatherland and, below, a German pillbox is toppled over by Red sappers. The Russians invaded East Prussia as early as October 24, according to an announcement by Stalin on that date, but the Reds were held to small gains throughout November and December. The big drive came on January 12 and Tannenberg fell on January 21.

PARATROOPERS BATTLE ELAS FORCES. After the invasion of Greece by the British on September 26, the war against the Nazis was complicated by Greek Civil War. Elas left wing forces were put down by British paratroopers in Athens. Here, the Tommies take cover behind a concrete pillar in Constitution Square and, below, they run to engage resisting Elas forces.

DRIVE ON THE BALTIC AND BALKAN STATES. The long Russian front bogged down in the center before Warsaw and the Soviets devoted the fall months to clearing their flanks of the enemy. They launched twin drives in the north and south, made peace with Finland; captured Tallinn and Riga on the Baltic; entered Belgrade October 20; signed an armistice with Bulgaria; encircled Budapest in December.

A TANK ACTION-THRILLER. Soviet tanks smash at enemy defenses on the right bank of the Danube, at an approach to Budapest. To engage the foe at closer quarters, Red tommy-gunners swarm from a tank turrett "on the double." Enemy fighting was stubborn at Budapest; Hungary did not surrender until January 21; and it was February before all resistance in the capital was quelled.

SOME ESCAPED—OTHERS DIDN'T. Hungarian troops fleeing before the Soviet forces near Budapest crossed the Danube River and wrecked this bridge behind them. Others, not so lucky, were trapped along with Nazi allies and marched through the mud and water to a Soviet rear area. The bitter fight for Budapest was waged over many weeks but the capital was completely encircled in December.

LANDING IS UNOPPOSED. On the morning of December 15 General MacArthur caught the Japs off-guard at Mindoro, in the Philippines, landing his assault troops without the loss of a man after convoying them 600 miles, almost always in sight of enemy land bases. A rocket ship softens up the coast line, above, in a twenty-minute bombardment wh'ch preceded the landings.

Crash landing at Mindoro December, 1944

THE PILOT WALKS AWAY UNHURT. Shaky but unharmed, this fighter pilot walks away from his P-38 after be'ng shot out of the sky by a Jap Zero over Mindoro Island. In the picture below, our ground troops march through San Jose as the natives smile their greeting.

Jap bombers fire an L.S.T. at Mindoro

THE CREW IS RESCUED. Flame and smoke billow from an L.S.T. (landing ship, tank) after a hit by a Jap bomb, but the crew, left, scramble aboard another ship after being snatched from the redhot deck of the stricken vessel. A destroyer pours water into the burning L.S.T. while a gun of another rescue vessel

looms in the foreground of the picture. Although the actual landings were made without casualties, the naval force suffered from repeated bombings made by Jap land-based bombers along the route of the convoy through the Surigao Strait past Mindanao, Cebu, and Palawan.

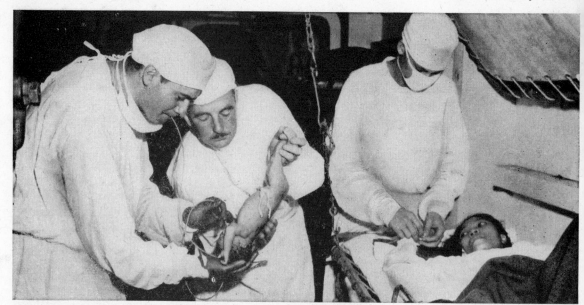

THE BEGINNING AND THE END. When a Filipino woman was brought to this L.S.T.'s sick bay after the invasion of Mindoro, the ship's doctors were able to deliver her of a baby girl. But they could not save a bluejacket who was injured when his ship was bombed by the Japanese and the crew sadly buries him at sea. The casket was draped with the American flag and services held.

RUSSIANS TASTE BREAD AGAIN. These Ukrainian girls, freed from forced labor under the Nazis, taste bread for the first time in many months. They were liberated from a German factory in Schirmeck by United States Sixth Army troops clearing the Vosges Mountains. At the right, freed prisoners carry a dead comrade from a German prisoner-of-war camp which was captured by Americans at Sarreguemines, France. Among the thousand men in the camp were Russians, Italians, Poles, and Frenchmen. Some of them had been in the hands of the Germans since the fall of Warsaw to the Nazis in 1939.

VON RUNDSTEDT COUNTER-ATTACKS. On December 16 Field Marshal von Rundstedt launched his first counteroffensive since Normandy, striking a major blow at the United States First Army front in Belgium and Luxembourg. The drive was undoubtedly the German bid to turn the tide. The finest troops, planes, tanks, and paratroops joined in the massive assault which sent our forces reeling back on a front fifty miles wide and which penetrated our lines an equal distance. These captured pictures show an enemy file going past an abandoned American jeep, top, and the remnants of an American supply train, right, are examined by a German soldier. Opposite page: enemy troops in action.

ARTILLERY AND ARMOR MEET NAZIS. Field pieces of the 101st Airborne Division dig in near Bastogne to throw shells at the German avalanche which poured into the Belgian Bulge. Below, light tanks of the American First Army rush forward to meet the German threat. Allied planes also hurled defiance at the Nazi counterattack when not grounded by bad weather.

YANKS PREPARE A HOT RECEPTION. When the German break-through came in the Belgium-Luxembourg salient, the Yanks lost no time in putting into effect counter measures. A mine-laying crew, above, conceals explosives along a road of the German advance and, below, an armored infantry battalion clears away burned-out gasoline cans, destroyed to deprive the enemy of the fuel.

The Battle of the Belgian Bulge

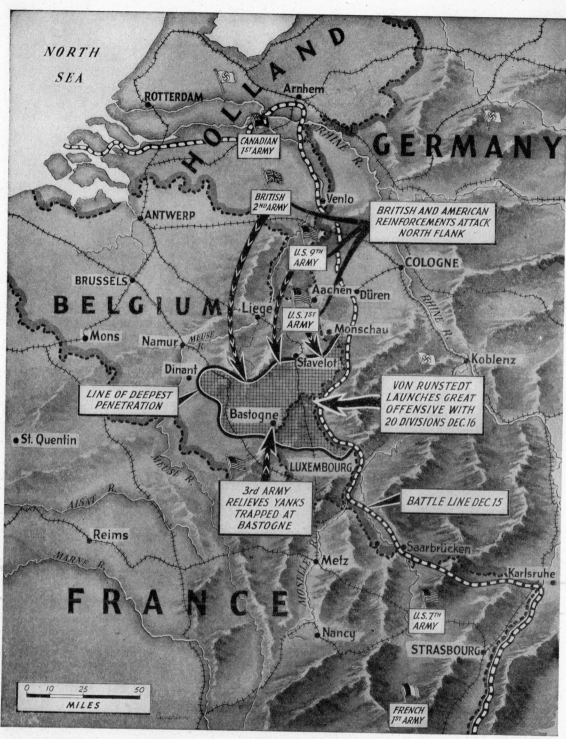

VON RUNDSTEDT COUNTERATTACKS. The Germans' one great effort to turn the tide of the Allied victories in Europe was their massive counterattack directed at the United States First Army lines in Belgium and Luxembourg. Von Rundstedt's divisions overran the shaded area of the map within a few days when the Allies brought them up short, struck at their flanks and ripped them from the air.

HE STAID BEHIND. Stavelot, taken early by the Germans in their lunge into Belgium, was one of the first towns to be retaken by the Allies. Heavy losses were suffered by both sides, the Nazi losses being mostly in men, the Allies losing principally tanks and guns. The picture shows one Nazi who fought his way into Stavelot and remained.

THEY WERE IN THE WAY. When the German juggernaut smashed into Stavelot, innocent civilians as well as soldiers were killed. Here an American soldier looks with silent sorrow upon the terrible price of war. The Allied flanks of the Nazi salient into the Belgium-Luxembourg lines held firm and it was pressure from the north and south that finally strangled the Nazi drive.

Victims of the German counteroffensive

December, 1944

THEY STOOD THEIR GROUND. American troops put up a gallant fight to stem the sudden, overpowering surge of the great German drive into the Belgium-Luxembourg salient. Five miles south of Bastogne, above, three American soldiers lie where they fell in the snow, while three other Yanks continue on the alert for the enemy. In the picture at the right, an American medical officer lies smothered in a landslide caused by an enemy bomb. Comrades go about the grim business of recovering the body. The enemy drive was short-lived but murderous.

THE YANKS SING CAROLS. Solemn-faced American soldiers raise their voices in Christmas songs at services held in the ruins of a house in La Gleize, Belgium, re-captured from the Germans by troops of the First Army. An Army Chaplain conducts the service in the eerie wreckage which is a reminder of the furious battle raging nearby.

BRITISH ARMOR ASSEMBLES. For the first time in the Burma campaign armor is assembled in strength between Kalewa and Shwebo. In the following three days the British column struck thirty miles through the jungle against determined Japanese resistance. While the Allies were meeting with success in Burma, the Japs continued their progress in China, seizing Tuyun, Chinese rail center.

YANKS SCORE. Doughboys attacking the northern flank of the Nazi salient into Belgium examine the bodies of dead Germans lying near their knocked out tank. Both British and American forces were diverted from the northern Westwall to come to the aid of the beleaguered First Army in the Belgium Bulge, and did much to turn the tide.

PLANES BRING AID. The gallant stand of the American force trapped at Bastogne was reinforced from the air. Here, C-47 transports fly over the battle zone with urgently needed supplies for the encircled Yanks who would not surrender. Smoke rises from German armor crippled on the battle ground. Planes were a big factor in lifting the siege of Bastogne.

Closing in on besieged Bastogne

THE YANKS ARE COMING. Infantry, armor, and engineers fight their way towards Bastogne and the besieged American unit which heroically would not give up to the encircling Nazis. Above, Yank infantrymen deploy in a field and inch their way toward the rescue of their buddies in the besieged Belgian town. In the right upper corner a mine sweeping unit clears a path for the attacking forces and, below, armored forces round up a group of German prisoners. A tank remains behind to guard the prisoners while other armor rolls forward to break the German trap forged around Bastogne. Meanwhile the surrounded division in Bastogne had been given an ultimatum by the attacking Nazis to surrender or be destroyed. The American commander's answer was "Nuts." On December 27 the Third Army smashed through the Nazi ring of iron and relieved the besieged defenders of Bastogne.

NAZIS SHOOT AMERICAN PRISONERS. In the outskirts of the village of Bausnez, near Malmedy, Belgium, the Nazis shot down American captives who had been herded into a snow-covered field during the Battle of the Belgian Bulge. Here, it is the unpleasant task of these Yanks to recover the bodies of their comrades. One Yank angrily sweeps aside the snow while another searches for identification.

BASTOGNE IS TAKEN. At the same time that General Patton's men broke the siege of Bastogne, the westernmost tip of von Rundstedt's push had also been blunted and the British and Americans were pressing down hard from the north. From then on it became a matter of systematically destroying the Bulge. The sulky and defiant Nazi prisoners shown here were taken in Bastogne.

BOOMERANG. American engineers early set out to counteract the Nazi flying bombs and United State factories were soon producing their own versions. Here, workmen of a motor company stack engine case of robot bomb jet propulsion engines designed to give the Nazis a dose of their own medicine. The engin is a copy of the German V-1.

The German genius for wrecking

NOTHING IS LEFT. The Nazi skill in destruction surpasses itself in the ripping up of this rail line in Latvia. Railways, because of their length, had formerly escaped complete wreckage, but the Nazis invented a device for going along miles of railroad and splintering the tough wooden ties like match sticks. A typical scene of desolation left by the Germans is the ruin in Rezekne, Latvia, pictured below. Whole blocks of the town were burned and demolished as the Nazis hurriedly retreated before the Russians.

ALL QUIET ON THIS FRONT. The last day of 1944 saw a temporary return to trench warfare on the British Second Army Front and the Tommy, above, has dug his machine gun nest in the frozen ground. However, Allied planes continued to hammer the enemy and the German soldier, below, lies sprawled amidst the wreckage of his flak wagon, now powerless to hinder the Allied sky offensive.

A NAZI SAYS "UNCLE". Carrying the white flag of surrender, this German soldier is seen from an American tank, a gun of which looms in the foreground of the picture. The captive was carrying a wounded comrade with several other medical corpsmen when the group gave up to American forces in Belgium. Appearing bedraggled and timid, the beaten Nazi bears a wound in the hand.

BURMESE JOY RIDE. Soldiers of the W.A.C. accompanied service forces to the far corners of the world in America's all-out global war. Here, two pretty Wacs take time out from their duties to view the Orient's strange sights from the backs of elephants, guided by a native boy.

RECONSTRUCTION BEGINS. Bastogne was a shambles when the Germans were chased out, but the Allies lost no time in repairing facilities so that the town could be used for an operations center. At the right, two Negro construction men of the Signal Corps go to work on mangled communications and, below, a couple of G.I.s go about their normal duties, using bicycles to make their way through the littered streets. After the Nazis were routed, they turned about and blasted the already flattened town with air attacks.

SALVAGED BY ORDNANCE. These metal monsters, crippled in battle, were recovered from the battle-fields and collected at this ordnance depot in France for repairs by technicians. Tanks which were too badly damaged to return to duty were salvaged for usable parts.

A PAGE FROM HITLER'S BOOK. The use of robot terror bombing forced Allied engineers to produce their own flying bomb. Here is the American improvement on the German V-1. In the top picture, smoke spouts from the undercarriage of a United States Army Air Forces buzz bomb as it starts up the ramp and, below, the bomb sheds its carriage and soars towards its target.

INVASION ARMADA AT LINGAYEN GULF. Under a protecting canopy of anti-aircraft fire, our forces moved into Lingayen Gulf on January 9 and the decisive battle was on for the Philippines. Despite the heavy anti-aircraft curtain and protection by planes of Admiral Kinkaid's Seventh Fleet, some Japs got through and inflicted damage on our ships and men. Below, a badly burned sailor enters a sick bay.

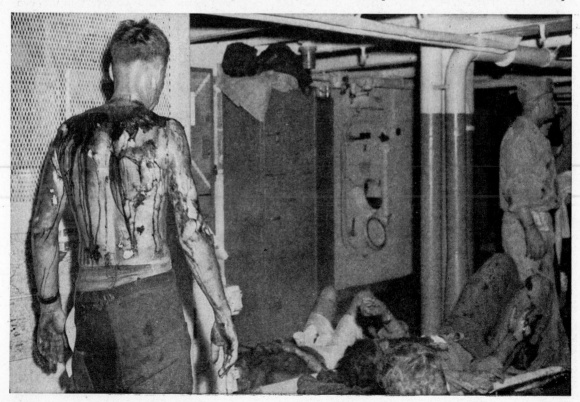

ROCKETS POUND THE BEACHES. Snapped in mid-air, these deadly rockets fly from an LCI (Landing Craft: Infantry) toward Jap positions on the shores of Lingayen Gulf at Luzon in the Philippines. General Walter Krueger's Sixth Army piled ashore on four beaches. In command of the attack forces was Admiral Thomas C. Kinkaid, below, Commander of the Seventh Fleet.

THE GERMAN BULGE IS DEFLATED. As winter settled over Luxembourg and Belgium, the Allies systematically eliminated the Belgian Bulge. White-clad British infantrymen hit the snow as a mortar shell bursts uncomfortably close and, in the picture below, British troops in Sherman tanks move up to support the Tommies in their attack on the German Ardennes salient in Belgium.

LOOKING FOR A FIGHT. United States infantrymen spread out and deploy as they move inland from Blue Beach looking for the little Japs who weren't there. Surprisingly light opposition was met at Lingayen Gulf but further inland, below, a Yank mortar team, harassed by Jap artillery, lashes back with mortar fire from a Filipino rice field where they were ambushed.

WINGED VICTORY LOOKS DOWN. Bedraggled citizens of La Roche, Belgium, stand beneath a World War I statue of Winged Victory and survey the ruins of their town. Driven from their homes by the Battle of the Belgian Bulge, they returned when the Germans retreated, only to find their homes a shambles. A few days later the shell of Houffalize, Belgium, was also liberated, below.

RUNS GANTLET OF FIRE. Our long supply lines were attacked not only in the waters of the Pacific but also at the landing beaches. This LST, packed with loaded vehicles, was subjected to severe Japanese artillery fire as it nosed up on the beach of Lingayen Gulf, Luzon. Much of the material, however, was gotten through to the men on the smoke-shrouded battle ground ashore.

THE FRENCH ADVANCE. Two stages of an infantry and tank advance against an enemy strongpoint are recorded by these photographs. In the top picture, French infantrymen and tanks are shown as they made a rush across an open field to assault the concealed position held by the Nazis. The smoke pall was probably laid down by the French to cloak the action. Below, the troops and armor have penetrated the wood and are pursuing the enemy over a swampy road.

CAUGHT IN AMERICAN UNIFORM. Grim Yanks force a Nazi prisoner at Geromont, Belgium, to take off United States Army shoes and pants which he was wearing. During the Battle of the Belgian Bulge many Nazis slipped behind the American lines, treacherously camouflaged in Allied uniforms. Since this wounded Nazi is wearing only part of the uniform, he may have done so for warmth.

YUM-M-M-M. United States Army C-ration tastes mighty good to this 20-year-old Filipino girl who was a member of the native guerilla forces for a year and one half. She carried a .38 colt automatic, was in several scraps with the enemy, and had two Japs to her credit. The Filipino underground forces were very helpful in smoothing the path of the American forces in Luzon.

ENGINEERS SWEEP FOR MINES. Engineers of the American 75th Division search a snow blanketed road for enemy mines before tanks move up to attack Commanster, Belgium. The snow made it difficult, too, for Belgian refugees, below, who carry their blanket rolls along the cold road back to the liberated town of Remmiville, Belgium. They fled from their homes when the Germans counterattacked in December.

GETTING ORIENTED IN THE C.B.I. THEATER. The Wacs accompanied our armed forces to the China-Burma-India theater to perform important services in support of the fighting. The Allies were faring better in the Burmese fighting, the British taking the important port of Akyab early in January. Here, Wacs ride in rickshaws and, below, remove their shoes before entering a temple.

BREAK-THROUGH. When the final big drive of the Russians erupted on January 12 between Warsaw and Cracow, the German defenses along the Vistula River were quickly breached. Above, Soviet troops force the Vistula under enemy fire and, below, infantry of the First Ukrainian Army fight to expand the bridgehead on the left bank of the river barrier. The drive quickly carried deep into Poland.

THE TOMMIES ATTACK. Infantry and armor of the British Second Army launched a new attack on the German salient between Roermond and Geilenkirchen, east of the Maas River, on January 16. In the picture above, the Tommies go after Nazi snipers and, below, infantrymen advance cautiously during fierce street fighting. Despite mud and snow, the assault gained local objectives.

VICTORY PROCESSION. Soviet horse-drawn artillery passes triumphantly through Cracow, above, and Soviet scouts, the first to enter the city, are greeted by the population, below. At the southern end of the long Russian front, the First Ukrainian Army also liberated Czestochowa and Radomsko in the first week of the final drive of the Soviets to break through to Germany and Berlin.

Polish troops parade in liberated Warsaw

VICTORY MARCH. Polish troops parade triumphantly through a ravaged street in Warsaw, liberated on January 17 by the Russians after over five years of occupation by the Nazi aggressors. Polish units helped free their capital.

THE BLOOM OF DEATH. The white blossoms are parachutes bearing bombs (parafrags) from American B-25s. One Jap plane is seen blown to bits while the camouflaged plane at the right escapes momentarily. The attack was made against enemy craft on the ground at Clark Field, important airfield which was taken by the Yanks January 25. Clark Field is about half way between Lingayen Gulf and Manila.

THE DISPOSSESED. With their meager belongings loaded in a cart, this family returns to its much
battered home in Warsaw, liberated by the Russians January 17. The wrecked city still smoulders. And,
below, a bedraggled family finds trees stripped of their branches by shell fire; their home a shambles.
Warsaw had been under siege by the Russians since the summer of 1944.

PULTUSK IN FLAMES. In the first electrifying days of the Soviet winter offensive hundreds of Polish communities were swept clear of the enemy. As the Second White Russian Army advanced north of the Polish capital it forged two bridgeheads across the Narew River, freeing Makow, Ciechanow, and Pultusk which is shown in flames as Red infantrymen storm forward.

CLOTHES COME OUT OF HIDING. During the long Japanese occupation of Luzon, Filipino women stored their good clothing away, but when the Yank liberators arrived the natives put on their gayest costumes to celebrate their freedom. These modish young women from Santa Barbara are looking their bashful best for the conquering American heroes.

A CARRIER BATTLES THE SEA. The Japs were not the only menace in the Pacific. Here, a huge aircraft carrier of the Essex class is tossed about like a tin plate in the heavy seas of a January storm. The ocean seethes and the atmosphere is blinding under the lash of a heavy wind.

The Reds enter Hungary's capital January, 1945

INSIDE BUDAPEST. Soviet troops have broken into the city and, although fighting is still going on, a Russian woman soldier calmly regulates traffic of vehicles and pedestrians. But the shooting continued and, in the picture below, Red Army men crouch behind a picket fence to fire their tommy guns at a Hitlerite strongpoint in the town's residential section.

ADVANCE IN THE SITTARD SECTOR. On January 16 the infantry and armor of the British Second Army launched an attack on a German salient east of the Maas River. A snow followed by a sudden thaw made it tough going for the men and vehicles. Also the Nazis resisted fiercely, but the British made good their initial objectives and cleared the area between the Juliana Canal and the Maas, following a link-up of British forces in that area. But the Nazis fought bitterly from the moment the British reached the Reich border and advances continued to be measured in yards during January. In these photographs, the Tommies are shown as they hit the snow and mud when German mortar bombs exploded too close for comfort.

GRIM BUSINESS ON LUZON. The Japs played the game of war for keeps, and few prisoners were taken. The above picture shows dead Japanese who were trapped in a ravine, and their American conquerors near Pozorrubio, Luzon. Below, two Jap tanks and their slain defenders litter a road near Binalonan. American tank destroyers accounted for the crippled Jap vehicles and their crews.

TANKS ASSEMBLE. Throughout the winter little progress was made below Bologna, but there was plenty of fierce fighting. Here, tanks assemble in a small Italian town and, below, infantrymen of the 85th Division move up to take their positions in the line where they relieved another company. They pass smoke pots which screen their movements.

OUTH TAKES A HAND. This young Russian tommygunner is greeted by a group of Lithuanian farm eople. In the harvest scene, below, a group of peasants raise their hands in friendly welcome and our their liberators a cooling drink. With the fall of Memel, Baltic seaport, on January 28, the libera- on of Lithuania was completed. Lithuania ceded Memel to the Germans in March, 1939, under pressure.

ON THE ROAD TO DEFEAT. This is a German bridge across the Nieman River, destroyed by the Naz in their retreat from Tilsit in East Prussia. The victorious Third White Russian Army entered the town shown below, as it still burned and smoked either from the Red attack or by the hand of the German themselves. At last the Nazis were being forced to take a dose of their own bitter medicine.

RECONNOITER FOR SNIPERS. Wearing winter camouflage, United States First Army troops flush a building in St. Vith, Belgium, for German snipers, above. The important road junction, below, was demolished in the heavy fighting for its possession. White-clad doughboys are still on the alert for remaining Germans. With St. Vith's re-capture, the Bulge became a blister.

The Ledo-Burma Road re-opens

CHINA'S LIFE ARTERY. Winding through jungles, over mountains, valleys and rivers, this is the Ledo-Burma Road. For two and one half years it could not be used due to a blockade by Japanese troops, but Allied troops cleared out the Japs, American engineers went ahead with construction work, and on

January 22 the Ledo-Burma Road was again ready to supply life blood to the heart of China. In the picture at the right, the first truck convoy to pass over the newly opened road assembles in Ledo, Assam, to travel with supplies to Kunming, China, approximately 1,000 miles distant.

OPPELN FALLS. In their lightning advance into German Silesia, the Russians captured Oppeln, bulwark of upper Silesia, on January 24. By the end of the month the entire Dabrowa industrial region was in the hands of the Soviets. In the picture above, Red tanks roll through the flaming city and, below, Soviet anti-aircraft gunners ward off attacks by German airmen.

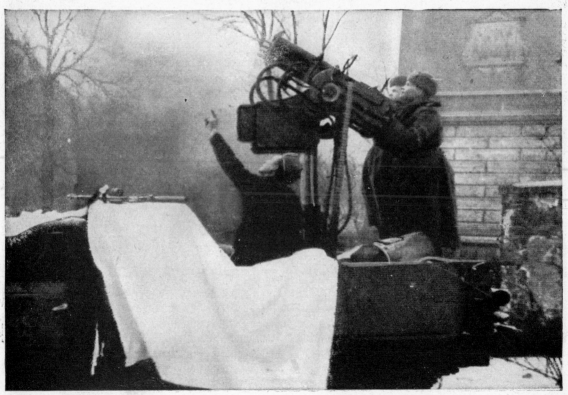

THE VOICE OF AUTHORITY. An eight-inch rifle rears up its muzzle to belch steel at German positions along the Westwall. The long, murderous barrel is camouflaged to blend with the bleak winter scene. Members of the gun crew, at the left, are adjusting the elevating mechanism.

RIP MANILA BAY FORTRESS. On January 24 land-based bombers of the Thirteenth Army Air Force in the Southwest Pacific struck at Cavite in Manila Bay. Cavite was destroyed by Jap bombs and American demolitions early in 1942, but the important naval base was completely rebuilt by the Japanese. The attack pictured here was the first by land-based bombers against Cavite.

BATTERING EAST PRUSSIA. The first great surge of the Russian winter offensive carried the Reds into East Prussia where they took the fortress city of Tannenberg on January 21 and Insterburg and Allenstein the following day. Russian artillery played an important role in the spectacular gains. Above, long range guns shell retreating Nazis in East Prussia. Below, artillery pounds Czech fortifications.

DANGER AHEAD. Commandos pick their way cautiously through the wreckage of this station, still under enemy fire, in Alsace. Note the tommy-gunner concealed warily in the doorway in the lower left hand corner of the picture. His buddies go forward as he covers them from his vantage point.

A GENERAL AND HIS MEN.
At the caravan headquarters of the British Second Army, Lieutenant General Sir Miles Christopher Dempsey, Commanding, studies a map with an Aide-de-Camp, right. The General launched a campaign on January 16 in the Sittard battle area between Roermond and Geilenkirchen. In the picture below, the General's men carry out the attack under cover of a crocodile flame-thrower along the road to St. Joost. The British took the town only after overcoming stiff enemy resistance.

AMIDST THE STRIFE OF BATTLE. In the murk and mud of the First White Russian Army front, a woman of the Soviet Army helps a severely wounded comrade. While Russian women did not play as large a part in active combat as sometimes supposed, they did perform miracles of courage and endurance in the nursing corps and other units of the Red Army.

RUN GANTLET OF FIRE. By the end of January, Field Marshall von Runstedt's thrust into Belgium had been turned back and the Yanks were again on the move against the Siegfried Line. Here, two Yanks dash forward under enemy shellfire in Mont Le Ban, Belgium. The house at the left has just been struck as the doughboys skirt the crumbled masonry, still smouldering from the hit.

A NAZI POCKET IS PICKED. Poznan in Poland and Breslau in Silesia held out in the rear areas long after the mighty Red armies had swept beyond, but the Russians left troops behind to hack at these pockets until their eventual capitulation. Soviet tommy-gunners and artillery men are shown dislodging the Nazis from strong points in the streets of besieged Poznan.

LOOKING FOR BOOBY TRAPS. German patrols continually sneaked into this British held town on the Western Front to lay booby traps. The British promptly organized counter booby trap patrols. As this British patrol goes on the prowl for the hidden explosives, the Jerrys let go with a bomb from a mortar and the Tommys hit the ground. The Nazis laid the booby traps under cover of nightfall.

DOWN TO THE SEA. Silhouetted against the sky, Russian tommygunners advance along the Baltic coast in the battle for Memel. Red Army men who were among the first to reach the Baltic Sea at Memel, captured January 28, are shown below. This port, unlike other Baltic seaports, never freezes, and is equipped with good docks and warehouses. The city was heavily fortified by the Germans.

RANGERS RAID CABANATUAN CAMP. General Douglas MacArthur's rangers made a daring raid on the Cabanatuan prison camp on January 30 and liberated many Americans right from under the noses of the Japs. Here, MacArthur talks to an old friend, Col. A. C. Oliver, who was among those liberated.

A FREIGHTER GOES DOWN WITH IT. The great floating drydock at Singapore, shown in the top picture as it housed a Jap freighter, was built in Great Britain and towed to Singapore. It could accommodate the largest battleship afloat. In the center photograph, a pall of black smoke rises from the drydock after it was struck by our bombs. The bottom picture shows the dock submerged and the freighter awash.

THRUST TOWARDS BERLIN. The great Russian offensive, begun on January 12, swept with electrifying speed across Poland and into German Silesia and East Prussia. Marshal Zhukoff's First White Russian Army poised a dagger point at the very heart of Germany, reaching the Oder at Kuestrin and Frankfort, only about thirty miles from the Nazi capital. Hundreds of Polish and German towns were swept up in the advance.

A Jap freighter gets its nose flattened

BOW IS BLOWN OFF. A B-26 of the Fifth Air Force swoops low to sow its deadly cargo in Pasaleng Bay, Luzon. Although two of the bombs explode wide of their target, one has already blown the bow of the

ship, right, to bits. Japanese landing craft are on the beach in the background and one of the bombs was probably directed at them.

The Americans seize Roer dams

AVERT FLOODS. Troops of the Ninth Infantry Division seized the above dam in time to avert Nazi demolitions which would have created flood barriers. Flood gates atop the Ruhrberg Dam, also on the Roer River, were blasted by the Nazis, below, and caused minor floods. The bomb craters near both dams were made by R.A.F. planes in December, 1944, when floods would have handicapped the enemy.

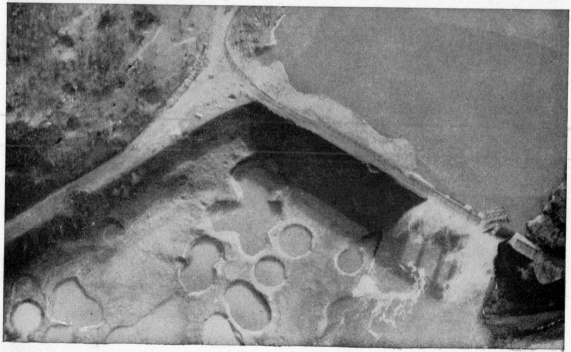

PASTING THE FATHERLAND. A Soviet big gun pounds after the Nazis fleeing over roads in their own East Prussia. The huge rifle is manned by men of the Second White Russian Army. Elsewhere in the north the Reds pierced to the Bay of Danzig, splitting the Germans on the Samland Peninsula, and in the south Breslau was ringed while other Russian forces swept beyond.

NOTHING IS SPARED. Four Yanks walk sadly through the ruins of a Catholic church which was destroyed as the barbaric Japs were driven from the Philippines. Only a remnant of the House of God still arches itself against the heavens. Three years of Jap rule worked many hardships on peoples of the Philippines.

Manila internees are freed

PRISON CAMPS ARE CAP-TURED. As American troops entered Manila, a part of the First Cavalry Division swooped swiftly down upon the Santo Thomas concentration camp, overcoming the garrison there and freeing hundreds of internees. Thirteen hundred and fifty internees were also released from Bilibid Prison in Manila, making a total of 5,000 Allied citizens liberated, of whom 4,000 were Americans. The picture at the right shows freed Santo Thomas prisoners getting a good American meal and the picture above shows Bilibid internees getting their first mail in over a year.

MAPPING DEFEAT FOR THE NAZIS. From February 4 to 11 the Big Three and their staffs met in an historic conference at Yalta in the Russian Crimea to chart the final defeat of Germany and to secure the foundation for a lasting peace. Above, Prime Minister Winston Churchill, President Franklin D. Roosevelt, and Premier Joseph Stalin. At the round table, below: Stalin and his aids, upper left: President Roosevelt with Admiral William D. Leahy, his personal Chief of Staff, and General George C. Marshall, Chief of Staff of the Army, upper right. Behind the cigar, lower left hand corner, is Prime Minister Churchill.

SIDELIGHTS AT YALTA. Above, Marshal Stalin and President Roosevelt get together for a heart to heart talk and, at the right, the Russian leader is amused as the British Prime Minister selects one of his ubiquitous stogies from a leather case. The war leaders and their staffs first discussed plans for final concerted military action against Germany and then turned their attention to problems of post war peace. The best military and diplomatic brains of the three great countries were assembled for the discussions which were held in the summer palace of former Czar Nicholas II on the Black Sea shore near Yalta in the Crimea.

THE TWAIN MEET. After the Yalta Conference President Franklin D. Roosevelt received Middle Eastern rulers on an American war vessel anchored in the Great Bitter Lake, through which the Suez Canal passes. In the picture above, the President is seen making a point to smiling Haile Selassie of Ethiopia and, below, he chats with King Farouk of Egypt.

Death in the streets of Manila

YANKS AND GUERILLAS BATTLE JAPS. Powerless to stop this grim American column, a dead Jap lies in the street before the pock-marked Far Eastern University building in Manila. Below, a Filipino guerilla takes command of a street by roping his ancient heavy caliber machine gun to a fire hydrant. A bamboo log serves as a front mount while the fire plug gives cover and concealment.

LARGEST OF ROER RIVER DAMS. The United States First Army's drive against the Roer River was held up temporarily by the swirling waters loosed when the Nazis blew up the flood gates of the Schwammenauel Dam, shown here. The dam is located east of Schmidt, a key strong point of the Siegfried Line. As the waters subsided, our troops seized control of the great dam.

TROOPS CROSS THE PASIG RIVER. American forces smashed into Manila on February 5, but the fanatical Japs put up a bloody fight within the city, burning and pillaging as they retreated. They destroyed all bridges across the Pasig River but the Yanks swarmed across the river in assault crafts. Here they are shown crossing the stream in hot pursuit of the stubborn enemy.

HE'LL ANSWER SOME QUESTIONS. Few Japanese were taken alive, but this fellow, minus everything but his life, was taken prisoner in the fierce street fighting in Manila. He's marched away at gunpoint to answer some questions. On February 6 the Eleventh Airborne Division entered the city from the south and the Thirty-seventh Infantry went in from the north. However, last-ditch Japs held out in Manila for many days, burning and looting as they fell back.

Carrier planes strike at Tokyo February 16, 1945

MORE BAD NEWS FOR JAP CAPITAL. For the first time, a full-scale carrier plane attack was launched against Tokyo on February 16 and 17. In place of the high flying B-29s, swarms of planes swooped in at tree-top level to bomb and strafe factories and other military targets in the Tokyo area. The planes were launched from a powerful task force of the Fifth Fleet close to the Japanese mainland. Fifteen to twenty of the fastest carriers were protected by destroyers, cruisers, submarines, and minesweepers in this daring blow at the heart of Japan. Twelve hundred planes of the United States Fleet participated in the devastating strike. The pictures show smoke rising from hits made on industrial targets.

The Yanks return to Corregidor

PARATROOPS DROP ON FORTRESS. Returning to the scene of America's most bitter defeat, skytroops drop down on Corregidor, island fortress in Manila Harbor. The island was first softened up by bombs from Army Air Force Liberator bombers which plastered the area mercilessly (picture above). It took American forces about two weeks to destroy the Japanese forces consisting of approximately 6,000 troops. On this tiny island American and Japanese forces fought from cave to cave and at the end of the month 4,215 enemy bodies had been counted. Our casualties were 136 killed, 531 wounded, eight missing. The foe fought to the point of annihilation with a force nearly double our own. They made repeated Banzai charges and had to be blasted out of the rocky caves and crannies or pushed into the sea.

Iwo Jima—Jap outpost in the Pacific

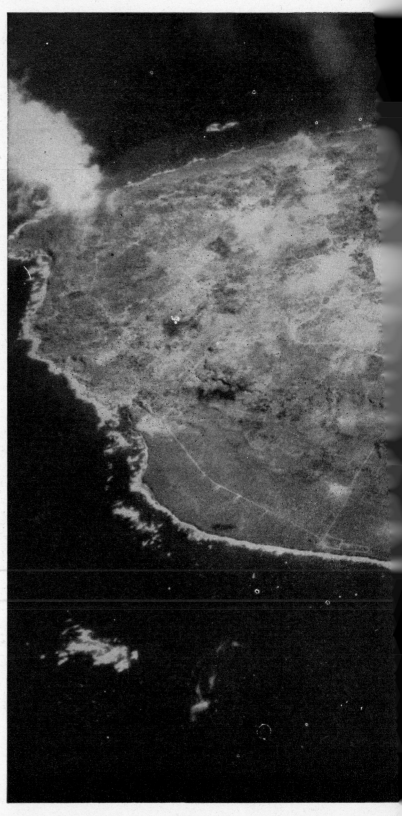

TOKYO'S DOORSTEP On the morning of February 19 the American Fourth and Fifth Marine Divisions invaded the tiny island of Iwo, one of the Volcano group, just 750 statute miles from Tokyo. Between thirty and forty thousand combat troops were borne to the scene of operations by an armada of more than 800 ships. Landings were forced at three places between the extinct volcanic core, Mt. Suribachi, lower right, and the projection of land at the top. Prior to the landings, warships circled the island, pouring a hail of steel into its defenses, and planes blasted the rocky fortress for seventy-two hours. Nevertheless, opposition was stiff and only after the bloodiest struggle were the marines able to carve out a beachhead 4,500 yards long and about 500 yards deep. The immediate objective of Lient. Gen. Holland M. Smith, commander of the troops, was the main airfield which was reached by patrols two hours after the initial landings.

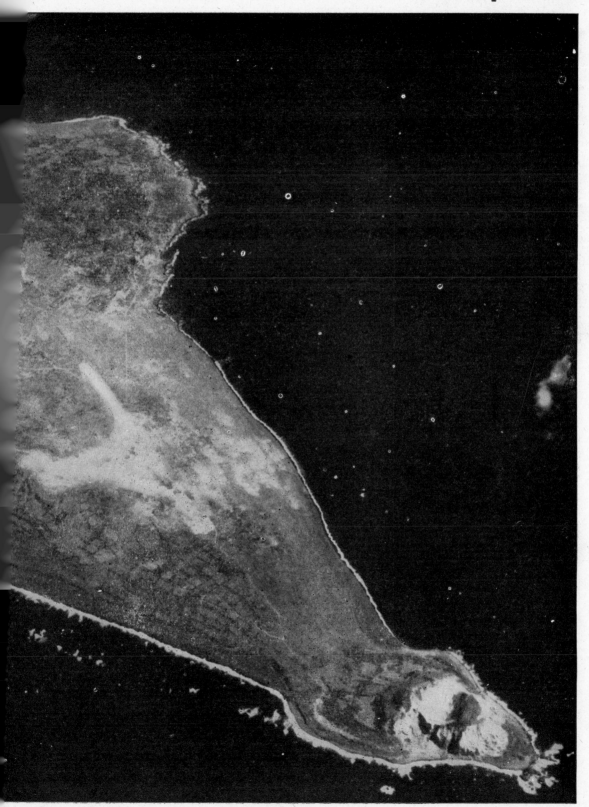

D-DAY BARRAGE. American marines forged their beachheads on Iwo Jima under cover of combined navy and air bombardments. A United States Navy LCS (Landing Craft, Support) is hurling rockets at the dug-in Japs. Despite the strength of the American covering forces, however, the initial assault was costly and fighting became more bloody as the struggle for the volcanic isle continued.

THE USS NEW YORK POUNDS ISLAND BASTION. For two days before the marines stormed Iwo Jima, battleships of the Pacific Fleet plastered the island with shells. Here, 14-inch guns belch smoke and fire as they pour steel into the enemy positions. At the end of the 48 hour bombardment, the USS New York moved in close to the Jap stronghold and blasted installations at point blank range.

On Japan's doorstep

February 19, 1945

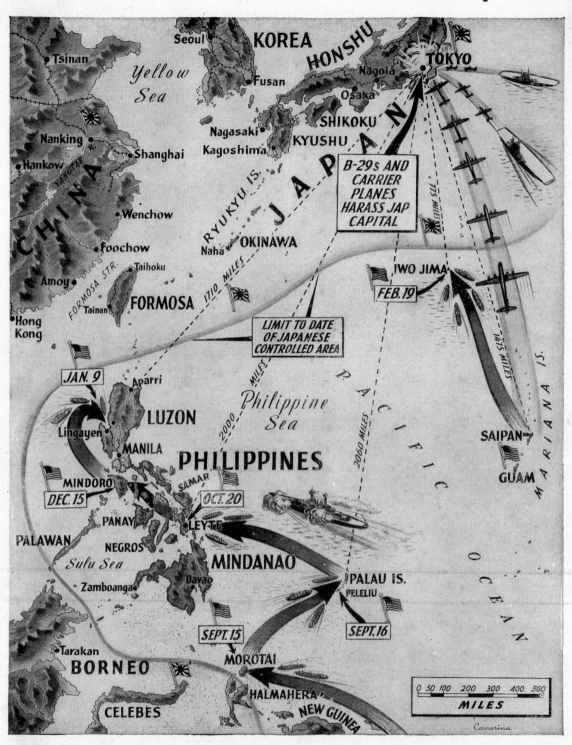

STEPPING STONES TO TOKYO. General Douglas MacArthur's long campaign of island hopping finally culminated in the dramatic invasion of Iwo Jima, less than 800 miles from Tokyo. From the Palau group in September, the Americans moved inexorably on to Leyte, Mindoro, Luzon, and then Iwo Jima. Simultaneously land and carrier based planes lashed Jap shipping and industrial targets.

Hitting the beach at Iwo Jima February 19, 1945

THE FIRST WAVE. Battle-tested marines of the Fourth Division assault the fire-raked beach of Iwo, above, and burrow into the sand, below, before pushing inland. This Division included veterans of every marine landing since Guadalcanal. The fighting was as bloody as any in the war. It was many days before the leathernecks were able to rout the fanatical Japs from this final stepping stone to Tokyo.

"KILLED IN ACTION." The invasion of Iwo Island was a bloody one and crews of landing craft were killed as well as assault troops. Here, Americans die at their gun post as enemy fire crashes aboard this LCI. Another ship puts alongside to assist the injured. Meanwhile, other assault boats were heading for the shores of Iwo.

INVASION WRECKAGE. Attesting to the bitter struggle of the Marines to get a foothold on Iwo's beaches, is this bleak shoreline littered with wreckage wrought by the fierce fire of the enemy. Landing craft were badly battered but the Leathernecks got ashore. Fighting troops may be seen on the beach and in the distance smoke rises from war gear still ablaze.

Mt. Suribachi—Gibraltar of the Japs

WE TOOK IT. Mt. Suribachi, at the southern tip of Iwo Jima island, is a rocky, extinct volcano. In its caves and crannies the Japs were hidden and heavily armed. The rugged "Jap Gibraltar" was captured, however, on D-day plus four. A four-man patrol of F Company, 28th Marines, ascended the volcano on February 23 followed by a platoon. But there was bitter fighting in the early days and the rock was first softened by naval and air bombardment. In this picture, Navy and Coast Guard LSTs swarm about the base of Mt. Suribachi as a naval rifle, in the foreground, directs its fire at the rugged crater of the formidable rock. Clouds of smoke rise as the shells burst about the base of the strong-point.

PUSHING INLAND. In the face of withering enemy fire, Fifth Division Marines inch their way up a slope from Red Beach One on the right wing of the invasion force. Below, a reserve wave of the Fourth Marine Division digs into the volcanic sand and awaits its turn to move up. A previous wave, almost invisible in the distant battle haze, charges ahead. Note the plane, upper right.

SUPPLIES POUR IN. Coast guard-manned and Navy landing craft kept a constant flow of supplies coming to the blackened sands of Iwo Jima. Food, munitions, war gear, and medical supplies were only a few hours behind the first assault waves. Here, landing craft are nosed up to the beach, their mouths gaping open, while soldiers carry and sort the growing heap of materials.

HOT SPOT. A blast of liquid flame is poured into the dugout of a die-hard Jap on Iwo Jima. A Fifth Division rifleman crouches in readiness to direct covering fire into the opening. Note the wounded American in foxhole. In the picture below, Jap fire is clipping the tree above the head of a Yank who charges forward over the body of a dead Nip.

"MAIL CALL." Letters from home were a powerful factor in the high morale of our fighting men and no effort was too great to get their mail to them promptly. Here, jubilant marines gather parapacks of mail dropped from a transport plane. Large quantities of blood plasma, necessitated by the high casualty rate, were delivered by the same speedy method.

MARINES PLANT THE STARS AND STRIPES ON MT. SURIBACHI. Just four days after D-day, this heroic group of marines of the 28th Regiment, Fifth Division, went up 550-foot Mt. Suribachi under enemy fire to raise the American flag. Other flags were raised on this blood-stained Pacific island and the formal flag raising did not take place until March 14 when Admiral Nimitz took over control of the island as military governor. However, this great picture, taken by Associated Press's Joe Rosenthal, was one of the most dramatic of the war.

WORDS, WORDS, WORDS. Scrawled by a Nazi propagandist on the walls of a building in Echt, Holland, are the brave words, "1918? Never again!" But United States Ninth Army Signalmen nevertheless go calmly about their business of putting up communication lines to get our own messages through. The first full-scale action in the Netherlands since October was begun early in February by the British and Canadians and the American Ninth Army. This was followed up by a full-scale Roer River offensive and the whole Western Front began to move forward. In the picture at the right, a holed-up member of the "master race" comes out of hiding to give up to an American officer near Linnich, Germany.

SEIZE BRIDGEHEAD. The United States First and Ninth Armies were successful in establishing a bridge-head across the Roer River in their large-scale offensive in February. Here, Ninth Army engineers of a combat battalion construct a foot bridge over the Roer near Linnich, Germany. By February 26 the Ninth and First Armies had merged their crossings into a solid 25-mile strip.

FROM WEST AND EAST. As the Russian armies hammered at the Oder River in the East, General Dwight Eisenhower set in motion a large-scale offensive towards the Rhine. Above, General Eisenhower, with cigarette; Maj. Gen. Raymond S. McLain, left, 19th Army Corps Commander; and Lt. Gen. William H. Simpson, U.S. Ninth Army Commander, right, confer in the German citadel of Juelich. Below, Col. Gen. Zakharov and Marshal Konev, leaders of Soviet armies, lay plans for an encirclement in the east.

The Yanks smash through Juelich

February 24, 1945

ON THE RHINE. Early in February the Allied armies began the preliminary movements in a large-scale drive to clear the western banks of the Rhine. On February 23 General Eisenhower launched a wide Roer River offensive and the vast offensive to the Rhine went into high gear. Here, Yanks of the United States march forward through a battered street in Juelich. Below, a dead Nazi and supply wagon.

STONE BY STONE. Russian infantrymen capture a block in the German city of Gleiwitz in Silesia during the rapid overrunning of that province. In the same city, below, the Reds ferret out Nazi snipers hiding in the rubble and ruin. The Soviet tide overflowed the rich Dabrowa industrial and coal area of Silesia in the first few days of the great Russian winter drive which was launched January 12.

FIRES RAVAGE CAPITAL. The dark blotches in this picture are part of the 240 city blocks burned out after 200 Superfortresses ripped Tokyo on February 25. The Ueno railroad was located in the dark section in the center. The giant air fleet plagued Tokyo from early morning until mid afternoon, giving inhabitants a full day of terror. The planes struck through a snow storm.

THE LAST STAGE. The elimination of snipers was usually the final phase of the conquest of any town. In Manila the Japs were particularly tenacious and after infantry and armored columns had freed most of the city, artillery barrages had to flatten the last remnants of resistance. Here, doughboys race to flush the Japs from their last hideouts in hand-to-hand fighting.

BATTLE OF THE CAVES. The Japs, fighting like wild men, had to be routed from the rocks and crannies of Iwo Jima by flames, grenades, and machine gun fire. Here, one Yank infantryman poises himself at the mouth of a Jap-infested cave while another Yank stands ready to back him up with a tommy gun.

B-29s RAKE SUPPLY DEPOT. As our Superfortresses ranged far and wide no corner of the Japanese stolen empire was safe. Here a load of bombs falls like snow over a supply depot near an airfield north of Rangoon, Burma. The big planes, operating in daylight from bases in India, started huge fires among ammunition dumps, and one column of smoke was seen rising to a height of 10,000 feet.

A bouquet of bombs for Muenchen-Gladbach   February, 1945

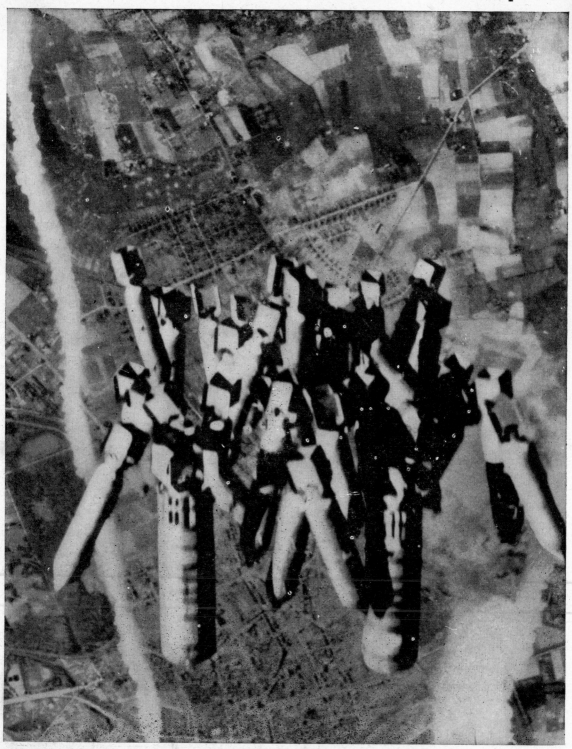

FUNERAL FLOWERS. This cluster of incendiaries and high explosives descended on rail yards at Muenchen-Gladbach as the Allies drove towards that large German city in February. In this particular attack 1,250 U.S. Army Eighth Air Force B-17 Fortresses and B-24 Liberators raided 11 rail yards to snarl German communications and seal off the industrial Ruhr from the rest of Germany.

The price for the Island of Iwo

THEY DIED FOR THEIR COUNTRY. Although American casualties were heavy on Iwo Jima, Admiral Richmond K. Turner and Lieut. Gen. Holland M. Smith, who led the invasion, said that five Japanese were killed for every marine who died. This would mean some 4,000 American deaths. In the first three or four days of the fighting alone, the rate of casualties was greater than at Tarawa or Saipan. In the first fifty-eight hours 648 Americans were killed, 4,168 wounded, 650 missing. For the same period, 1,222 Japanese corpses were counted. The enemy fought fiercely for every inch of this tiny, blackened volcanic island in the front yard of their homeland.

Mountain troops advance in Italy

WITH THE FIFTH ARMY. Enemy dead line this road in Italy as the Fifth Army's Tenth Mountain Division moves grimly forward to capture an important road junction. The column of infantry was closely sup-

ported by artillery and fighter bombers. At the right, engineers of this same division rest in the rear of a tank destroyer which offers some protection from enemy sniper fire.

VICTORY IN EUROPE

ARLY in March the Allies began their climactic march to victory in Europe by aching the Rhine River defenses at Rema-1. The United States First Army seized the lendorff Bridge on March 7 in a spectacular p just ten minutes before the Nazis had nned to blow it up. Troops and armour red across and established a bridgehead the east bank of the Rhine—the first in-ders to cross the river barrier since Napo-n in 1805.

The Germans, by frantic shelling, knocked t the Ludendorff Bridge on March 17. But was too late—the bridgehead was firm and pontoon span was already in use. To the rth and south of the First Army's break-rough even greater catastrophes were be-lling the Wehrmacht. Marshal Sir Bernard ontgomery's 21st Army Group had trapped e German forces west of the Rhine in the rth and in the vicinity of Wesel an Allied rborne army of 40,000 troops crossed the hine on March 24. At the southern end of the ont, Patton's Third and Patch's Seventh Army ere enveloping the Nazi forces in the Saar iangle between the Rhine and the Moselle iver and by the end of the month the entire llied front had pushed across the Rhine.

On the east bank of the Rhine the advance ecame a blitzkrieg. Tanks plunged deep into he Reich, planes rained devastation on owns and communications, confusion spread hroughout Germany. By the middle of April he 12th Army Group had encircled and liqui-dated more than 300,000 enemy troops in the Ruhr industrial region. The United States Ninth Army captured Hannover on April 11 and the British Second Army was fighting in the out-skirts of Bremen. The Seventh broke into Nurenberg on April 17—the Third Army was veering toward Czechoslavakia, and the First outflanked Leipzig. The German forces were thrown into chaos, cut into fragments and by-passed. On April 25 the Allied sweep cul-minated in the junction with the Soviet forces at Torgau on the Elbe River and the Reich was cut in two.

The final crack-up in Germany started on May 4 when all the forces in north Germany, the Netherlands and Denmark surrendered to Marshal Bernard Montgomery's 12th Army Group. Almost simultaneously the Russian and Italian fronts were cracked wide open and on May 7 Germany surrendered uncon-ditionally to the Supreme Allied Command at Rheims, France, after five years, eight months and six days of the greatest conflict in history.

THE RUSSIAN CONTRIBUTION

WHILE the great Allied offensive was roll-ing into the Reich from the west, the Russian forces were exerting immense pres-sure on the eastern front. Halted momentarily at Kuestrin on the Oder in the center of their line, the Soviet armies pounded at the north-ern and then at the southern end of the line, alternately. Marshal Rokossovsky's Second Russian Army was pressing large German forces into the upper end of the Danzig Cor-ridor; far to the south other Soviet forces were battling toward Vienna.

In mid-April Marshal Zhukov's mighty forces of some million and one-half men lashed out again toward Berlin even as the Allies were fast approaching the German citadel from the west. The suburbs of Berlin were gained. At the same time Marshal Konev's forces to the south had broken loose and were pushing for a junction with the United States First Army in the vicinity of the Elbe River.

On April 25 the Russians linked-up with the Allies at the Elbe and on May 2 the furious battle for Berlin was won. These two shatter-ing events were followed by the complete collapse of Germany. The unconditional sur-render of the German forces at Rheims, France, on May 7, was ratified on May 8 by the Rus-sians at Berlin.

THE NAZI COLLAPSE IN ITALY

THROUGHOUT March the stalemate in Italy still held, but early in April General Mark W. Clark, commander of the Allied armies in Italy, declared: "The final great battles for the liberation of Italy and the destruction of the German invader have started."

At last the Fifth Army had broken out of the Apennines and on April 22, with Polish troops of the Eighth Army, took Bologna, major Allied objective since the fall of 1944. With the capture of this important transportation center, the whole Po Valley became vulner-able, and Allied troops swept into the broad plains in a great breakthrough that engulfed Genoa on April 27 and Milan on April 29. The Germans were retreating under heavy straf-ing all along the lines. The Fifth Army raced pell-mell towards France, the Eighth Army was forging a trap along the Swiss border and New Zealand troops made contact with Yugo-slav patriots near Trieste.

The Germans no longer had an organized army in the field in Italy and there was for Col. Gen. von Vietinghoff, commanding German forces in northern Italy and western Austria, nothing to do but surrender unconditionally. This put one million troops of the Nazi war machine out of the hopeless fight less than a week before the complete uncon ditional surrender at Rheims, France.

THE POLITICAL FRONT

IN the last six months of the war there took place sensational political events which were closely related to the battlefronts. America's war leader, President Franklin Delano

Roosevelt, died on April 12; Adolph Hitler v reported dead on April 1; Benito Mussolini i an ignominious death by Italian partisans April 28. In England, Clement Atlee was vo by Labor to succeed Prime Minister Wins Churchill. But, important as these chang were, they did not halt the high tide of ever An attempt to insure a lasting peace after war was made by the United Nations Conf ence at San Francisco and the Big Three n at Potsdam to hasten the inevitable end of t war and also to plan a basis for an enduri peace after hostilities.

VICTORY OVER THE JAPANESE

WITH the end of the war in Europe the full power of the Allies was at once directed at Japan. Redeployment of troops had, in fact, begun even before the unconditional surrender of Germany.

The grim fight for Iwo Jima had ended on March 14, except for small pockets of resistance, and the American flag was formally raised. Meanwhile amphibious assaults had been made against Mindanao, March 11, and Panay, March 18, both important islands in the Philippines. The heavy air and naval attacks continued; Admiral Mitscher's Fifth Fleet trapped the Japanese Home Fleet in the Inland Sea, inflicting heavy damage and carrier planes and bombers supplemented the ground and sea attacks with devastating raids from the China Sea to the home islands.

The invasion of Okinawa in the Ryukyus on April 1 was the last major battle with the Japanese. It raged for three months during which time the American forces waged day and night warfare by land, sea and air. It was not until the end of May that Shuri and Naha, key strongpoints, fell to the Marines. By June 21, Okinawa was conquered. More than 90,000 Japanese had been killed; 4,000 taken prisoner.

The battle for Luzon in the Philippines, invaded early in the year, was waged all through the spring and into the summer. The campaign ended on June 27 after the 200-mile Cagayan Valley had been overrun in twenty-eight days, the operation costing the enemy over 100,000 dead.

While these major battles were being fought, campaigns were also carried out in Borneo, Burma, and China. The Borneo Islands were invaded in three successful operations: Australian troops landed on Tarakan, May 2; other landings were made June 10; and Balik

Papan was stormed on July 1. These success cut the Japanese forces in two in the Ea Indies.

The important Burma campaign was vi tually at an end with the capture of Rangoc on May 3 by American, British, Chinese, Afr can and Indian troops. The Japanese in th three year campaign in Burma suffered 347,00 casualties, 97,000 of which were counted deac

As Burma was cleared of the Japanese, th Allies were also able to make progress i China. The important air base of Liuchow wa recaptured in June and the Japanese wer being pushed back all along the line.

While the land campaigns were everywhere going against the Japanese, the air and sec attacks relentlessly increased in power anc tempo and in July our warships so dominatec the Pacific that they were able for the firs time to shell the Japanese homeland at point blank range. Meanwhile the air arm of the fleet as well as Superfortresses and B-29s pummelled Japanese cities at will.

The battle for Japan had reached its final phase; plans were in readiness for the invasion of the home islands themselves. As it happened, the invasion took place without a shot being fired. On August 6 the first atomic bomb was dropped on Hiroshima and an already beaten Japan knew that her fate was sealed. A second atomic bomb dropped on Nagasaki seemed superfluous to a stunned world. Russia quickly declared war on the Japanese on August 9 and the reeling Japanese offered to surrender to the Allies. Hostilities ceased on August 14.

The subjugation of Japan was completed on the last day of the sixth year of World War II when the instrument of surrender was signed, September 2, aboard the U.S.S. Missouri in Tokyo Bay.

The Allies drive to the Rhine
March, 1945

The Allies drive to the Rhine

March, 1945

Legend
- START OF OFFENSIVE
- BATTLE LINE
- GENERAL DIRECTION OF DRIVES
- SUPER HIGHWAYS

AMERICAN 9TH AND CANADIAN 1ST JOIN FRONTS MAR. 3

AM. 9TH REACHES RHINE RIVER MAR. 2

AM. 1ST & 9TH ARMIES ATTACK AT ROER FEB. 23

AMERICAN 1ST CROSSES RHINE AT REMAGEN MARCH 7

AM. 3RD DRIVES FOR COBLENZ MAR. 3

AM. 3RD ATTACKS FROM MOSELLE LINE

ALLIED POSITION FEB. 23

AM. 7TH ATTACKS ON WIDE FRONT

BATTLE LINE

HOLLAND · BELGIUM · FRANCE · GERMANY · LUX.

0 10 20 30 40 50
MILES

Cannina

CLEAR GERMANS FROM WEST BANK. Early in March a great Allied offensive was relentlessly pushing the Nazis back to their last natural barrier, the Rhine River. The American Ninth and Canadian First Armies linked up in the north, Patton's Third Army struck from the Moselle in the south and the First Army in the center staged the most spectacular success by crossing the Rhine at Remagen on March 7.

TOWN IS CRUSHED. Although the Twenty-ninth Division of the American Ninth Army took Muenchen-Gladbach with a loss of only five men, the town itself took a battering from Allied bombs and shells as these pictures testify. To the north the Canadian First Army was crunching ahead through fierce resistance to link-up with the Ninth Army.

BRAZILIAN NURSES ATTEND WOUNDED. Infantrymen of the Tenth Mountain Division pass a dead German as they dash over the crest of a hill in the Appenines below Bologna. The Nazi was killed by artillery fire. Members of the Nurse Corps of the Brazilian Expeditionary Force, below, helped to attend the sick and wounded at the 16th Evacuation Hospital, Pistoia area, Italy.

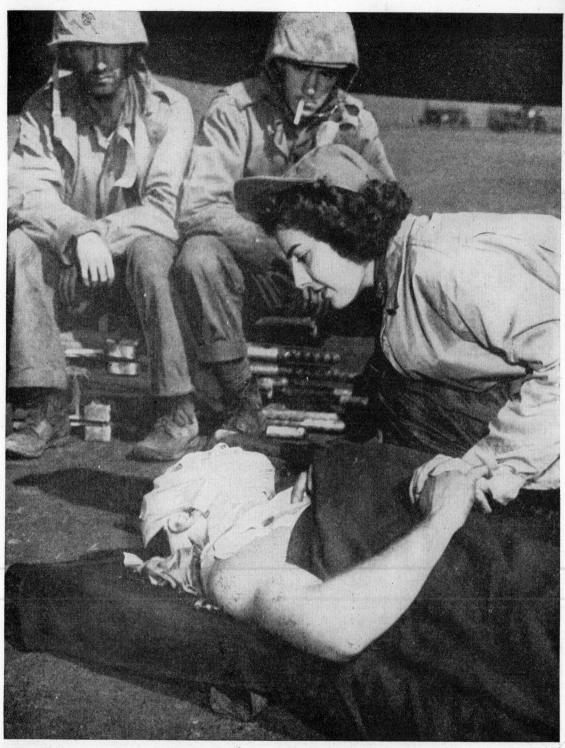

FIRST ON ANY BATTLEFIELD. Ensign Jane Kendleigh of Oberlin, Ohio, was the first Navy flight nurse to set foot on any battlefield. Here, she attends a wounded man on the airstrip at Iwo Jima. The nurse's plane landed on the island under mortar fire and, before it could evacuate sixteen wounded men, there was a delay of eighty minutes while planes finished an attack on nearby enemy positions.

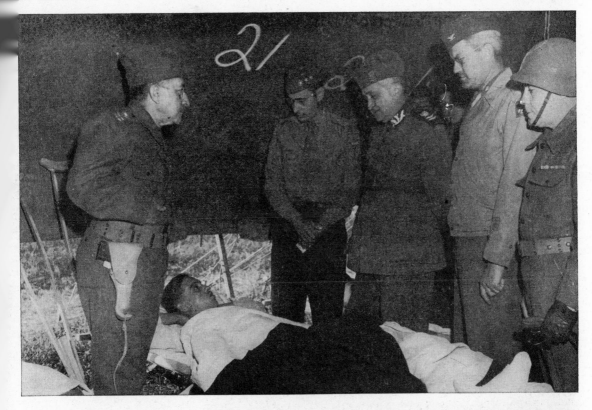

HIGH OFFICIALS HONOR BRAZILIAN G.I.s. The Brazilian Expeditionary Force played an important part in the fighting in Italy. Above, a wounded Brazilian soldier is visited by high officials and, below, General Mark Clark, Commander of all United Nations troops in Italy, decorates a Brazilian soldier for bravery. Standing in the upper picture are, left to right: Maj. Gen. Joao Batista Mascarenhas de Moraes, Commanding General of the BEF; Major Ernistino Oliviera, senior Brazilian Medical Officer at the 38th Evacuation Hospital; General Eurico Gaspar Dutra, Minister of War of Brazil; Colonel George T. Wood, of High Point, N. C., Commanding officer of the 38th Evac.; and Col. Marcus Porto, chief medical officer of the BEF.

The First Army captures ruined Cologne

CATHEDRAL STILL STANDS. With the fall of Cologne all of the west bank of the Rhine to the north, with the exception of small pockets, was brought under Allied control. Large sections of the once beautiful city were utterly destroyed, with the cathedral the only building not severely damaged. Twenty-five large scale aerial attacks spread 42,000 tons of bombs on the city, causing destruction far exceeding that wrought by the enemy on London. Two thirds of the city's built-up area was wiped out. To the south of Cologne other American units were closing in on the river and Bonn; Patton drove to within twenty miles of the Rhine and Coblenz; and to the north the United States and Canadian First Armies were breaking down the Wesel pocket.

The U.S. First Army crosses the Rhine

SEIZES BRIDGE AT REMAGEN.
Veterans of the United States First Army captured the Ludendorff Bridge at Remagen and established a bridgehead across the Rhine in one of the war's great dramatic coups. The vital bridge was seized in the nick of time, just ten minutes before the Germans planned to blow it up. Immediately, American troops began to pour across the Rhine by the thousands. Not since 1805, when Napoleon's forces from the English Channel coast swept across the Rhine to rout the Austrians at Ulm, had the Rhine been crossed by an invading army. In this picture the captured bridge is shown with houses destroyed on the west bank and smoke from shelling arising from the eastern bank. With this breaching of the Rhine the heart of Germany was exposed. It was the beginning of the end.

MEN AND SUPPLIES CONTINUE TO CROSS RHINE. The Germans frantically tried to knock out the Ludendorff Bridge but it was too late—the Yanks continued to cross under heavy fire and succeeded in widening and strengthening their bridgehead. Crippled American jeeps are shown in the top picture and, below, men and jeeps enter upon the bridge as anti-aircraft crews ward off air attacks.

HELL'S CORNER. Not only the railroad bridge at Remagen but also the town of Remagen was subjected to heavy enemy shelling but infantrymen of the First Army moved in an endless stream into the city. Below, they advance along a shore road towards the town, and enter the town, above. The doughboys keep close to the buildings for protection against the steady artillery pounding.

The Nazis blow their bridges behind them

FAIL TO STOP THE YANKS. All along the Rhine the Nazis were withdrawing in frantic confusion to the east bank, destroying their own bridges in their wake: the Hoenzollern Bridge at Cologne, left; the bridge at Bonn, above; and the Adolph Hitler Bridge, below, at Uerdingen. But someone slipped up at Remagen and the fatal breach was made. Elsewhere the Allies flew across the Rhine and even built their own bridges.

NAZI PRISONERS. The German soldiers herded together, above, were taken in the outskirts of Breslau in German Silesia. Below, one captive Nazi smiles for the Russian photographer. The main Russian drive was stopped momentarily at Kuestrin and Frankfort, but the Silesian campaign drove forward, threatening Cottbus southeast of Berlin, and to the north the Soviets menaced the German seaport of Stettin. Severe fighting also raged in Hungary where Budapest fell on February 13 after which the Russians swung toward Vienna.

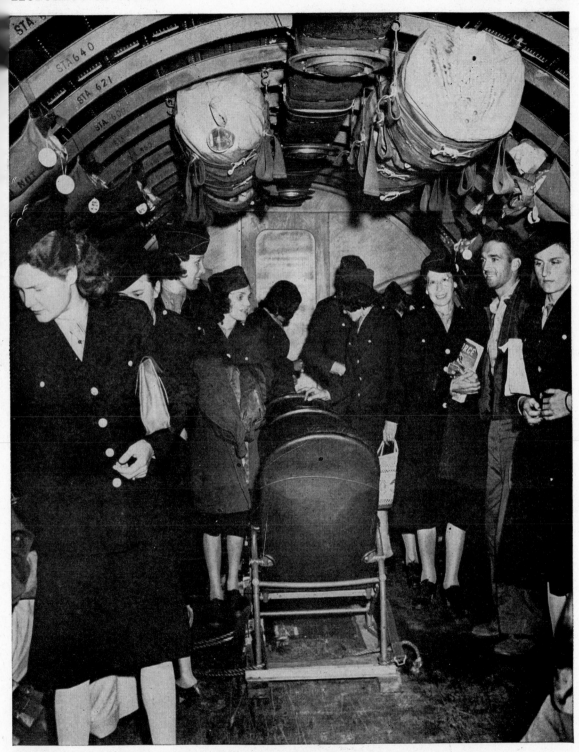

HOMEWARD BOUND. Navy nurses, rescued from Las Banos internment camp at Luzon in the Philippines, debark from a Naval Air Transport Service plane at Honolulu. Wan from their long ordeal in the Jap prison camp, the girls are bound for the states and a rest. They are wearing Army uniforms which were picked up in the forward area.

THE YANKS ROLL THROUGH SPEICHER. As the Nazis crumbled everywhere west of the Rhine, the Allies chased them relentlessly back across their last great natural defense line. The enormous power of the Allied push is indicated by the wreckage of this German town through which roll tanks and infantry of the Third Army. Overwhelming air power supported the ground forces.

GERMAN HOSPITALITY. After the 11th Armored Division of the Third Army smashed into Andernach, Nazi snipers protested with pot shots. In the top picture, the doughboys have spotted a sniper and raise their rifles to get him. Below, two Nazis give up and hold their hands behind their heads as the Yanks go on in for others hiding in the houses.

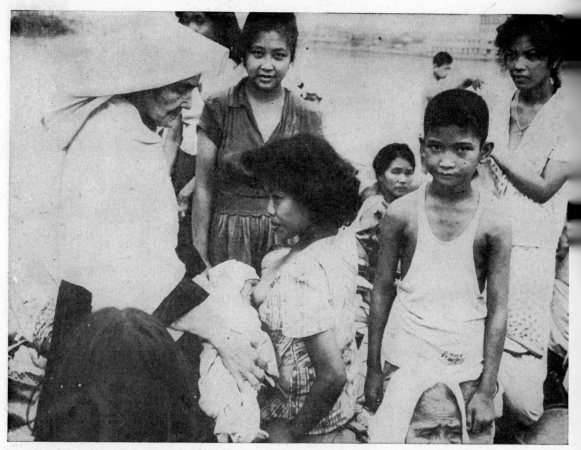

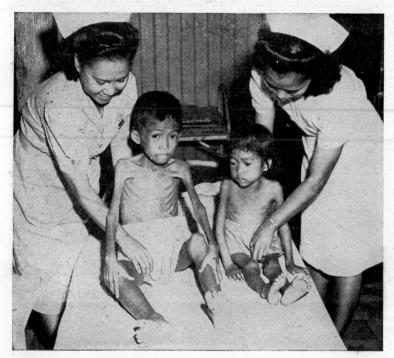

CHILD VICTIMS. Assisted by a nun, this young Filipino mother feeds a two-day-old orphan of the fighting in Manila. The girl holds her own baby under her arm as she nurses the foundling. In the picture below, children suffering from malnutrition are cared for at a Tablac hospital on Luzon Island in the Philippines. The nurses are native volunteers. Hardship to civilians was particularly severe in Manila where the Japs not only held out in house-to-house fighting but also pillaged and destroyed as they retreated.

BLOCK BUSTER. Neither natural obstacles nor man-made barriers could stop the Allies in their sweep to the Rhine River in Germany. Here, a powerful United States Army tank has plowed through a roadblock and two Nazis lie dead as a Yank comes up to take a look. The whole Allied front was chewing up every remnant of the German armies west of the Rhine.

16.7 SQUARE MILES ARE OBLITERATED. After 300 B-29s raided the Japanese capital on March 9, the heart of Japan looked like this. Mile upon mile of buildings in the industrial area had to be wiped out in order to destroy the many small sub-contracting facilities. Only by the use of incendiary bombs could this widespread arsenal for Japan's war machine be effectively eliminated.

CLASH WITH NAZIS NEAR WALDAU. Infantrymen of the 26th Division splash through the chilly waters of the Schleuse River, after first covering their advance with machine gun fire. The Nazi SS trooper sprawled in the water was caught by a burst of the machine gun and the Yanks drive forward to assault German troops dug in among the surrounding pine forests.

U.S. Eighth Army troops speed for Mindanao

ATTACK SECOND LARGEST ISLE OF PHILIPPINES. Veterans of the 41st Division, Eighth Army, borne by Navy landing craft of the Sixth Amphibious Group, streak for the shore at Zamboanga on the southwest tip of Mindanao, main Jap bastion at the southern end of the Philippine archipelago. Prior to the invasion, the landing area was pounded for ten days by cruisers, destroyers and gunboats of Rear Admiral Russell Berkey's division of the Seventh Fleet and the final blow, bottom picture, was struck by three squadrons of heavy bombers of the Thirteenth Air Force. Some mortar and machine gun fire was met by the landing craft but none of the boats was hit and the green clad troops went ashore standing up. The 41st Division of Lieut. Gen. Robert J. Eichelberger's Eighth Army was led by Maj. Gen. Jans A. Doe on a 1,400 yard stretch of beach.

BERLIN IS THREATENED. Afte thirty-five days of battle, th Reds stormed into Kuestrin, ke fortress on the route to Berlir thirty-eight miles to the wes Above, Soviet machine-gunner rage through a German hel street in Kuestrin and, below they walk with guns aler through a street that has bee: cleared of the enemy. Germa: snipers were always left behin to slow up their pursuers. Par of the city of Kuestrin lies on th west bank of the Oder River.

A TOUGH NUT. Breslau was ringed and penetrated early in the great Russian winter offensive but a stubborn core of resistance held out until the end of the war with the Russian forces sweeping beyond and leaving rear-guard troops to mop up. The Germans erected barricades like the one above and bitterly contested every house. Below, Soviet tommy-gunners spray a hail of steel at an enemy strongpoint in a shell-torn street. Another town which held out long after the Russian forces had sped beyond was Poznan, Polish city on the route to the Oder and Berlin. Poznan capitulated on February 23, however, while Breslau was being contested right up to the last days of the war.

Freed Russian slave laborers meet Nazi "boss"

REVENGE IS SWEET. When the University city of Bonn was captured by the First Division on March 10 many slave laborers were relieved of the Nazi yoke. The Russians pictured here had slaved for the Nazis in a factory for three years. After their release by the Yanks they were looking for a Displaced Persons Center when whom should they meet but their former Nazi master, now a civilian policeman. First, upper left, they relieve the "boss" of his bike. Then one angry Red belabors him with a brief case, lower left, and another comes to close grips with the Nazi, right. In the last scene, below, the Nazi sprints hurriedly away, looking fearfully over his shoulder at the pursuing Russians.

THE W.A.C. GOES SIGHT-SEEING. Four members of the Women's Army Corps, among the first to arrive in Luzon, are driven through the streets of Manila in a native cart after talking the driver into giving them a lift. Our women soldiers performed invaluable services in the Pacific theater.

END OF A BLOODY BATTLE. The Japanese practice of hiding in caves, tunnels, and subterranean retreats, availed them nothing in the fight for Mandalay which fell to the British on March 20. These bullet-riddled Japs were trapped and exterminated in this stone tunnel in Mandalay, capital of the last Burmese dynasty in the center of the dry zone of middle Burma.

THE LAST BARRIER TO BERLIN. In the mighty Soviet winter offensive, the Reds lunged to the banks of the Oder River in less than a month of fighting. On the banks of this natural obstacle the Russian forces paused, but by March they had forged beachheads on the other side of the Oder at Kuestrin. Above Soviet guardsmen are shown capturing a bridgehead and, below, signalmen report from the west bank

SCANNING THE EAST BANK. An observer of the United States Ninth Army perches on the terrace of a building on the west bank of the Rhine and sizes up German positions on the other side. By the end of the month the whole Western Front had pushed over to the eastern shore and was fanning out over Germany against light opposition by the disintegrating Nazi forces.

LINE UP FOR INSPECTION. Navy men, wearing Army khaki, line up for drill during the training period prior to crossing the Rhine. Navy personnel and craft were used extensively in getting our armies successfully over the water obstacle to the inner Reich. The Navy men shown here were attached to the Ninth Army and were stationed near the Meuse River in Belgium.

PRIZE OF WAR. These doughboys of the United States Ninth Army get a drink of beer the hard way. First they had to capture a German fort near the Rhine. The Ninth Army stormed across the Rhine during the great Allied offensive which cracked the northern end of the Western Front at the end of March. Note the shells in the foreground of picture.

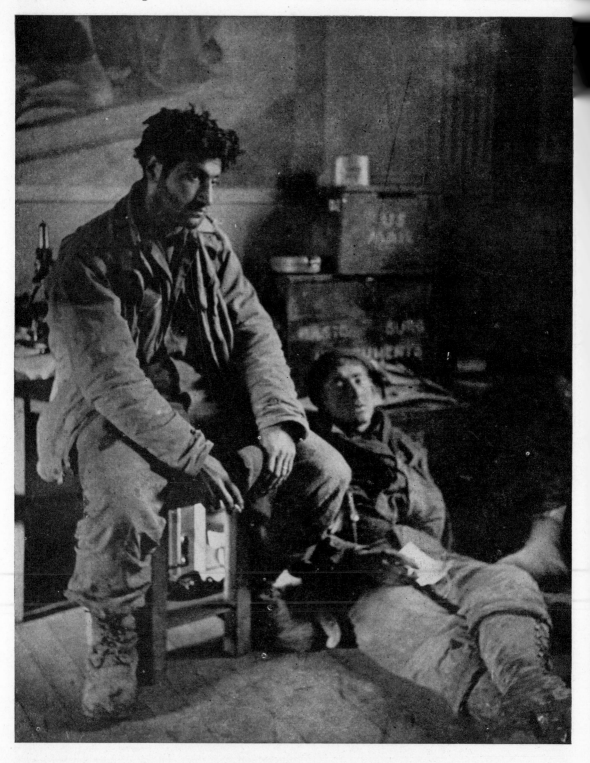

WAR WEARY. Caked with mud, these doughboys rest between battles. Their eyes and faces are heavy with fatigue as they take time out for a smoke. One holds a letter from home in his lap.

HEAD FOR COBLENZ. Infantrymen of the United States Third Army cross the Moselle River in assault craft, above, and jeeps are ferried over in their wake below. A few days later General Patton's rampaging army was storming the Rhine and smashing deep into Germany.

BOMBERS SHATTER INDUSTRIAL TARGETS. Raids on the Japanese capital became more and more frequent both by carrier based planes and B-29s. Carrier based Navy warbirds spread the destruction shown here in the very heart of the city's industrial area. Smoke towers from row after row of shattered and wrecked war production factories.

ENGINEERS ARE PLUNGED INTO RHINE. After ten days of frantic shelling by the Germans, the Ludendorff Bridge across the Rhine at Remagen collapsed. Hundreds of engineers were working on the bridge when the west end caved in, pulling the east end, below, from its mooring. American First Army medics rescued many of the men who were on the bridge at the time of its collapse.

Paving a path across the Rhine

OBLITERATION BOMBING.
Wesel, Germany, focal point of American forces which crossed the Rhine north of the Ruhr Valley, is a mere mud-hole after large-scale bombing attacks by American tactical air forces. The bombings were followed up by a vast airborne invasion by 40,000 troops. Note the railway track in the foreground, gouged and torn from its bed, while two cathedrals still stand, upper right, indicating the pin-point accuracy of Allied bombing.

PANAY IS PUSHOVER. Within 60 hours after United States forces hit the beaches of Panay, above, the small Philippine bastion was ours. Preliminary work of Filipino guerillas expedited the victory. Below, Army forces take cover from snipers as they move inland.

DEATH OF A HERO. Killed by a German sniper hidden on the east bank of the Rhine River, an American soldier lies on the walk of the Ernst Ludwig Bridge, spanning the Rhine at Worms. Two other Yanks are alert to avenge their buddy. Units of the United States Seventh Army later crossed the water barrier in this area and stormed into the city of Worms.

The Franklin survives in tragedy at sea

DEATH TOLL IS HEAVY. When a Japanese dive-bomber dropped two heavy bombs forward and aft on the decks of the U.S.S. Franklin, the 27,000-ton carrier burst into a raging inferno, but her valiant crew pulled her through and brought her 12,000 miles to the Brooklyn Navy Yard for repairs. But before the battle was won 832 of the crew had given their lives and 270 were wounded in the heroic fight against almost impossible odds. Captain Leslie E. Gehres said that practically every member of the crew had been a hero. Groups of men were trapped in flaming compartments below deck and others were forced to one end of the upper deck by the heat and flames (upper left picture). Even the gun turrets, upper right, burst into flames. In the picture at the lower left, members of the crew, circle, wait to be rescued, and at the right the Santa Fe comes along side to assist in the fight. The huge carrier was hit sixty miles off main Japanese islands.

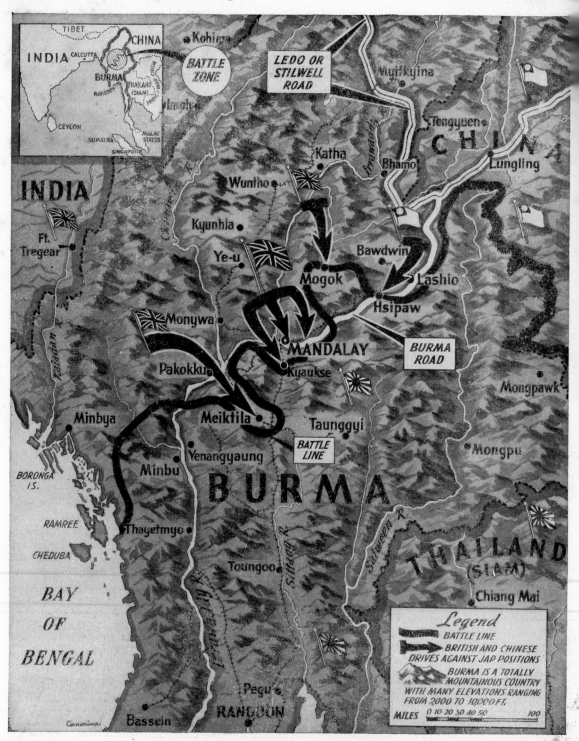

CUT UP JAP GROUPS IN CENTRAL BURMA. After almost three years of Japanese occupation, Mandalay fell to the British on March 20. Throughout central Burma, Japanese forces amounting to perhaps 25,000 troops were being carved up by Allied Fourteenth Army troops. Mogok was captured. The Chinese were mopping up Hsipaw and a British block was established at Meiktila, 80 miles south of Mandalay.

BRINGING THEM IN ALIVE. The Japs are not given to surrender but these fellows were trapped in the jungle near Mandalay and nabbed before they could commit hara-kiri. The fall of Mandalay had great political importance since it was considered by the Burmese as the focal point of national life. Of greater military importance was the capture of Meiktila to the south.

Infantrymen bag S.S. trooper

CAUGHT WHILE FLEEING. Yanks of the 104th Division, First Army, stand alertly over the body of an S.S. trooper who tried to get away from them by fleeing across a field. The platoon below, with the same fighting outfit, captured 24 S.S. troopers near the German town of Scherfede. All members of this platoon were volunteers with the First Army.

A SECOND BRIDGEHEAD IS FORGED. Jeeps and armor of the 87th Division, United States Third Army, speed across the Rhine to establish the second American bridgehead on the east bank. The German armies west of the river barrier were almost completely destroyed or driven to the east bank. By March 25 the whole Allied front had pushed over the Rhine.

LINES ACROSS THE RHINE. A cable is laid across the Rhine River at Boppard, Germany, by United States Third Army signalmen, above. Armored elements are ferried across, below, to back up the infantry. The signalmen in the top picture are working with the assistance of a Navy LCVP. The Third Army made sensational gains east of the Rhine, racing thirty-two miles to the Main River.

THE ROAD OUT. When the Third Army stormed across the Rhine on March 22 they were not held to their bridgehead for long as the dead Germans sprawled along this road east of the Rhine testify. Two columns raced with electrifying speed into the interior of Germany reaching the Main River and Frankfort, while other columns joined the First Army near Giessen.

Two "master men" are captured

GIVE WAY TO GRIEF. The Nazi soldier, in the pictures above, bids goodbye to his wife and child over the railing of a temporary prisoner cage before being sent off to a prison in the rear. Below, a 16-year-old Nazi, captured by the United States First Army, starts to cry, left; turns away, center; and at the right sobs and leans against a wall.

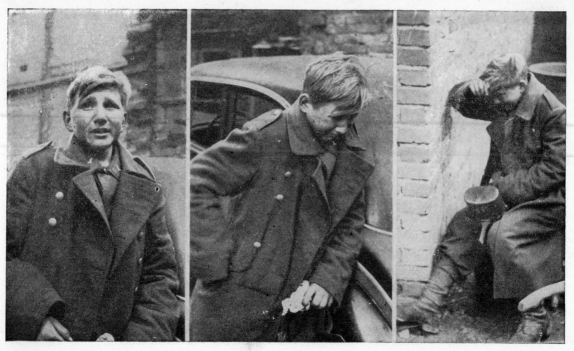

BIG GUNS AND ARMOR MOVE UP. British medium guns line up near the Rhine, above, in preparation for the great Allied offensive north of the Ruhr on March 24. Below, British mechanized equipment moves through a town on the Wesel-Geldern road as they push forward toward the Rhine River at the northern end of the Western Front. An Allied Airborne Army crossed the Rhine simultaneously.

TROOPS JUMP ACROSS THE RHINE. Glider troops of the First Allied Airborne Army leave their plane and prepare for enemy resistance near Wesel, Germany. They are part of 40,000 troops that participated in a large scale air invasion east of the Rhine. This was the largest operation of its kind at the time. Below, troops gather into units for the mass airborne attack east of the Rhine.

SKYTROOPS DROP IN. When 40,000 troops of the First Allied Airborne Army were dropped east of the Rhine near Wesel, German civilians found the war taking place in their back yards. The civilians above watch operations placidly while the mother and children, below, take refuge in a foxhole to avoid the shooting. Note the parachute draped from a tree in the top picture.

BACK AIRBORNE ATTACK. When 40,000 Allied airborne troops were dropped on the east bank of the Rhine near Wesel, they were separated from their supplies by water, but materials were flown over by the United States Army Eighth Air Force. Here a B-24 Liberator sends battle supplies parachuting down to points where they will be picked up by airborne units.

MANEUVER FOR OKINAWA. The Karama Islands off Okinawa's southwest coast were quickly taken by troops of the 77th Division. Doughboys are shown going inland on Tokashiki where they set up a base to cover landings on Okinawa soon afterward. The conquest of this group resulted in the capture of more than 300 "suicide" boats, below, wh_ch were designed by the Japs to ram American ships.

SURGE OUT OF RHINE BRIDGEHEAD. Armored forces and infantry of the British Second Army went on a rampage at the northern end of the Western Front, breaking out of their bridgehead east of the Rhine and streaming into the Westphalian plains. In the picture above, Tommies advance along a road littered with German dead and, below, a Scottish division looks on as Nazi captives march to the rear.

THE RUSSIANS ENTER BALTIC PORT. Danzig, Baltic port which was at the center of the dispute which touched off World War II, was entered by Russian troops late in March. The great seaport is shown blazing furiously as the Soviets forced the Germans out. The seizure of this city by the Russians virtually wiped out a large segment of the Baltic front.

MANY PREFERRED SUICIDE. A large number of Japanese civilians in the Karama Islands, invaded as a preliminary to the Okinawa landings, took their own lives rather than be captured. American troops rounded up the remainder and gave them medical care, food and water. Jap soldiers machine-gunned our troops as they removed the civilian wounded. The group shown here was taken on Tokashiki Island.

DEFEATED NAZIS. As the United States First Army broke out of its Remagen bridgehead, it moved so fast in a "rat race" with the fleeing Germans that the front was more than 100 miles in advance of headquarters. Thousands of prisoners were taken while those who preferred to fight were being exterminated between the First and Ninth Army fronts. The prisoners shown here preferred not to fight.

OFFENSIVE IN POMERANIA. Red Army motorized units rumble forward in the direction of Stettin, important German seaport on the Baltic, and, below, Red infantrymen file through a flaming and shattered street in Daber. In March three great prongs of the Russian offensive were stabbing toward the Baltic in the north; Kuestrin and Frankfurt in the center; and Cottbus to the south.

BOUND FOR BERLIN. A Red tank rolls along the great modern motor highway towards Berlin while a Soviet gun crew pulls up to one side to take care of some enemy opposition. Every inch of the way, however, had to be fought for and it was not until April that the Russian armies were able to batter their way into the fanatically held capital of Germany.

AT A DISPLACED PERSONS CENTER. Men and women civilians who were used by the Germans as slave laborers line up for food at a center for displaced persons in Germany. Among them are Poles, Frenchmen, Russians, Belgians and Czechs, freed by the Allied Armies pouring into Germany.

LAND ON RYUKYU ISLANDS. Soldiers and marines of the American Tenth Army stormed the south-west shore of Okinawa after first making landings on the smaller islands to the west. The ships on the map show the direction of these two operations and the aircraft carriers indicate the support of Admiral Mitscher's carrier planes. The inset map pictures the relation of the Ryukyus to the Jap home islands.

An Easter greeting for Okinawa

KNOCKING AT TOKYO'S DOOR. The guns of Admiral Spruance's Fifth Fleet cut loose at Jap installations on Okinawa on Easter Sunday, April 1, as the Twenty-fourth Army Corps and the Marine Third Amphibious Corps stormed ashore against negligible opposition. Landing on the west coast of Okinawa, which is 362 statute miles from the home islands, the troops quickly worked inland to seize Yontan and Katena airfields. It was the largest amphibious operation ever carried out in the Pacific up to that time; more than 1,400 ships were in the armada; carrier and land-based planes as well as superfortresses participated. The Twenty-fourth Army Corps was under Maj. Gen. John R. Hodge and the Marines were under Maj. Gen. Roy S. Geiger. Inexplicably the Japanese abandoned their strong coastal defenses and retired inland where they later fought with their usual fanaticism.

The Yanks land in the Ryukyus April 1, 1945

BEACH PARTY. The Okinawa landings were practically uncontested, to the amazement of leathernecks who had fought on the blood-drenched beaches from Guadalcanal to Iwo Jima. Inland, however, the fighting was as bitter as any in the war. In these pictures marines are shown making their initial landings. Army troops also participated in the landings as did naval personnel.

IT LOOKS GOOD TO THEM. These high ranking American generals in Germany are exultant over the spectacular success of their armies plunging into the interior of the Reich. Left to right, they are: General Dwight D. Eisenhower, Supreme Allied Commander in Chief in the European Theater; Lieut. Gen. George S. Patton, Jr., Commander of the United States Third Army; Lieut. Gen. Omar N. Bradley, Twelfth Army Group Commander; and Lieut. Gen. Courtney Hodges, U. S. First Army Commander.

MARCH OF FREEDOM. It was a glorious Easter Sunday morning for these smiling, flag-waving, singing Frenchmen who were freed from a German prison camp by a cavalry reconnaisance unit of the United States Ninth Army. The Ninth Army, with the First Army, was exterminating the massed German armies trapped between the two American forces and the Rhine River.

ON THE ROAD TO NUREMBERG. As this Nazi ran across a street in Wuerzburg to hurl his potato masher at advancing Allies he was chopped down by an infantryman of the 42nd Division. The Seventh Army pushed across the Main south of Wuerzburg to reach Bad Mergentheim and advanced fifteen miles southeast of Mannheim. Other units had only forty-four miles to go to reach Nuremberg.

Nazi generals surrender to G.I.s

April, 194

THE WEHRMACHT TOTTERS. Two high ranking German officers, who were in charge of Hersfel
drive up to surrender to a couple of tough looking Yanks in a tank of the Fourth Armored Divisio
United States Third Army. Three thousand tanks were rolling across the Reich, smashing a path t
the six great Allied armies in the west, stabbing ever deeper into the vitals of the Reich.

THE WHEEL OF CHANCE. Luck was not with one Yank who lies dead beside a wagon wheel in the German town of Oberdorla. Another doughboy takes a chance against Nazi sniper bullets and two more await their turn. The town was captured by infantry and tanks of the Sixth Armored Division, Third Army. A 300-mile arc of 1,000,000 Allied troops east of the Rhine was moving to eclipse Germany.

ENOUGH! Waving the white flag of surrender, these Nazi small fry in Hesselbach, try to give up to onrushing Seventh Army soldiers, but the Yanks are too intent on the retreating German Army to pay much heed. Another point in the path of the Allies was Limburg, bottom picture, now reduced to a twisted mass of wreckage by Allied bombings. Debris is remains of marshalling yards.

A STRIKE. An American B-25, its nose painted grotesquely, swoops down on a Japanese escort vessel to send it to the bottom of the China Sea. The bomb bays are still open. The Nipponese vessel went down soon afterward. In other forays in the same area, B-25s sunk a Jap warship similar to the type shown here. Superforts continued to pound the homeland.

PATTON HITS JACKPOT. One hundred tons of gold bullion and millions in currency and art treasures were uncovered in a salt mine near Merkers by troops of General Patton's Third Army. An American finance officer, left, checks the money bags with a Reichbank official. The colossal cache was revealed to military police by two gossipy German women.

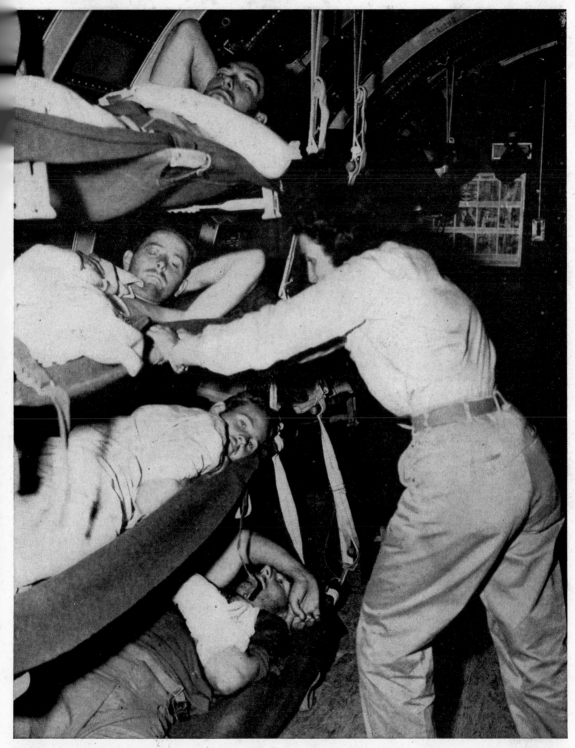

RACE AGAINST TIME. Speedy hospitalization saved many lives of American troops on Okinawa. After being given first aid on the battlefield, the more serious cases were put aboard huge transport planes staffed by capable nurses and doctors. Here, a flight nurse secures a casualty into his stretcher aboard a transport which has been converted into a hospital plane after bringing in supplies.

THE YAMATO IS SUNK. The 40,000 ton battleship, Yamato, again tries to flee from American planes, above, but in this engagement she was sunk as well as two cruisers and three destroyers. Three other destroyers were left burning. Jap planes struck back and the United States Navy anchorage threw up a heavy barrage, below. The Japs got decidedly the worst of the battle.

ERNIE PYLE AND BUDDIES. The foot soldier's correspondent, Ernie Pyle, shares his cigarettes with some First Division marines as they rest at an Okinawa roadside. Pyle, more than any other writer, told the story of the common G.I. A few days after the scene shown here, Pyle was instantly killed by a blast of Japanese machine gun fire on Ie Jima.

Naval guns hurl steel at Okinawa

A DOSE OF DYNAMITE FOR THE JAPS. The camera, quicker than the eye, caught these 16-inch shells (circle) as they soared to their distant target on Okinawa. A huge burst of fire and smoke

spurts from the guns of the battleship and the terrific repercussion sets up a streak of foam in the water at the ship's sides. After putting ashore invasion forces, the fleet battered land targets.

ADVANCES AGAINST RIFLE FIRE. Rushing across an open field raked by small arms fire, Seventh Army Infantrymen assault the blazing town of Hulirich which was first shelled. Only thirty-four miles from Nuremburg, the Seventh Army was running into strong resistance as it battled across Bavaria. The town of Crailsheim was seized and thousands of Germans faced entrapment.

KOENIGSBERG FALLS. Led by a pistol waving non-com, these Red infantrymen charge through a street of Koenigsberg which had resisted the Russian onslaught for weeks. In the battle-scarred street, below, tanks overrun enemy positions. Koenigsberg was a key fortress for the Germans on the Baltic coast and its collapse presaged the general German disaster in that sector.

PENETRATE TO HEART OF CAPITAL. Vienna, second largest city of Hitler's "Greater Germany" was virtually in the hands of the Russians as they stormed into the center of the old capital. Furious Soviet tank and infantry assaults had carried into the famous city from a siege arc of ninety-eight miles. The picture shows the Uranian building and the Aspern bridge, wrecked by retreating SS troops.

FORMER CHANCELLOR IS CAPTURED. The sportily attired gent sitting grimly in the garden, above, is Germany's former Chancellor and envoy to Turkey, Franz von Papen, who was nabbed by American Ninth Army glider troops in the Ruhr pocket. Upper right, he talks to his captors, and in the picture below, he is questioned by Maj. Gen. Harry L. Twaddle. Von Papen's son is at the left.

MORALE BOOSTER. The ranks of the American armies contained many able professional entertainers who were organized into units to lift the spirits of the fighting troops between battles. Here, Pfc. Mickey Rooney gets broad grins from Yanks of the Seventh Army. As the Allied armies rolled over the Reich in pursuit of the Germans, entertainment units followed along with laughs and songs.

A BRIDGE IS BUILT IN TEN DAYS. Erected with metal girders made in Luxembourg and wooden piles cut from German forests, this bridge was thrown across the Rhine at Wesel in just ten days by Allied engineers. A permanent railroad bridge, it sped supplies to the Allied forces sweeping across Germany. Although plans called for construction in two weeks, the bridge was actually completed two days ahead of schedule. The devastation in the lower picture is what remained of Hamm, railway nerve center northeast of Essen, after its capture by the United States Ninth Army.

ALLIES LIBERATE CONCENTRATION CAMPS. Elaborate torture chambers, gallows, and crematories (pictured above) were found by the Eightieth Division when it captured the Buchenwald concentration camp near Jena, Germany, on April 10. The pitiful remains, below, were found by the Third Armored Division when it entered the Lager Nordhausen, concentration camp, at Nordhausen, Germany.

UP AND AT 'EM. The marines launch an attack from behind a small ridge on Okinawa Island in the Ryukyus. In the picture above, the marine at the left carries a radio and the leading man lugs a roll of communication wire as well as full combat gear. Below, the leathernecks hold their rifles ready and the marine in the center carries a flame thrower. Note also entrenching tools and grenades, in hand.

FRANKLIN DELANO ROOSEVELT: JAN. 30, 1882-APRIL 12, 1945. The death of the Commander-in-Chief on April 12 at Warm Springs, Ga., stunned and grieved the nation and freedom-loving people all over the world. He died of a cerebral hemorrhage as the European war neared its climax and was denied the joy of victory that he had fought so hard for. He was the nation's thirty-first president and the only four-time Chief Executive. The picture here shown was his last formal portrait.

HARRY S. TRUMAN TAKES OATH. Raising his hand solemnly, Harry S. Truman is sworn is as President of the United States by Chief Justice Harlan Stone in the executive offices of the White House, Washington, D. C., April 12. Mrs. Truman witnesses the ceremony, behind her is Secretary of State Edward R. Stettinius, Jr., and behind the new president is Attorney General Francis Biddle.

THE NATION'S CAPITAL PAYS HOMAGE. A seventeen-car train bore the body of the late President from Warm Springs, Ga., to the capital where flags were at half mast and the populace was hushed with grief. Formal funeral services were held at the White House after which the body was taken to Hyde Park for burial.

GERMANY DISINTEGRATES. After crossing the Rhine early in March, the Allied armies in the west quickly exploited their break-through, plunging with incredible power and force into the very heart of Germany. The sweeping advance of the Allied armies is indicated by the arrows. Together with the Russian forces in the east, the Allies were rapidly squeezing Germany into the shaded portion of the map.

1885

"Between the crosses, row on row"

AN AMERICAN CEMETERY IN BELGIUM. German prisoners of war, assigned to grave digging, trudge through the large American First Army cemetery near Henri Chapelle, Belgium. More than 15,000 Americans had found their last resting place here by March; by May American casualties on all fronts were nearing the million mark.

THEY DON'T LIKE IT. After the fall of Schweinfurt, ball bearing center in Germany, male civilians between the ages of sixteen and sixty were rounded up to be checked by American authorities. Their faces show that it's a bitter pill for the "master race." After the conquest of this town, the United States Seventh Army raced on, making giant strides across Bavaria.

BEYOND THE REACH OF BOMBS. In a salt mine near Engels, Germany, United States Ninth Army troops found these nearly completed Heinkel jet planes, capable of a speed of 650 miles per hour. The assembly line, 300 meters beneath the earth, was reportedly in operation for several months with an output of 40 or 50 planes a month. A large elevator brought planes to surface.

MASTERPIECES WENT UNDER-GROUND. The famous painting "Winter Garden," by Edouard Manet, above, was found in a salt mine vault at Merkers, Germany, by the United States Third Army. The priceless Reubens, below, was found in a cave at Siegen, Germany, by troops of the First Army. Within a few weeks Allied occupation forces found 500 hoards of paintings, documents, books, and statuary, a great amount of it stolen from Holland. Public collections were confiscated as a matter of course by the Nazis; private collections were "sold" under pressure.

BAD NEWS FOR GERMANY AND JAPAN. Announcing that aid would be extended to our Allies until the "complete defeat of Germany and Japan", President Harry S. Truman (seated), puts his signature to the third extension of the lend-lease act. Witnessing the signature, left to right, are Rep. Charles A. Eaton, N. J.; Sen. Tom Connally, Tex.; Oscar Cox, counsel, Foreign Economic Administration; Leo Crowley, Foreign Economic Administrator; Secretary of State Edward R. Stettinius, Jr. The United States provided $39,000,000,000 of lend-lease aid in four and three-quarter years, Crowley later revealed, and received in reverse lend-lease $5,600,000,000.

Thousands of Nazis are trapped in Ruhr pocket

STRONGHOLD IS CUT IN TWO. The encircled German troops in the Ruhr, far behind the fast-driving main armies of the Allies, were cut in two in mid-April when troops of the American First and Ninth Armies met at Wetter. The bag of prisoners was enormous. The Nazi captives shown in this picture are part of 82,000 taken by the Eighteenth Airborne Corps near Gummersbach. General Omar N. Bradley, Twelfth Army Group Commander, stated that 316,930 prisoners had been captured during the liquidation of the pocket and that the final figure would surpass the record number of 330,000 Germans killed or captured in the battle of Stalingrad. The general said that he had used seventeen divisions, or 240,000 men, in reducing the Ruhr, a number at least equalling that of the German defenses. Many high ranking Nazis were included in the bag. Since crossing the Rhine, the general said that his Twelfth Group's First, Third, Ninth and Fifteenth Armies had taken 842,864 prisoners.

A NIP IS COOKED. The leathernecks set fire to this thatched shack on Okinawa to rout out a Jap sniper. The Nip never did come out though and the marines waited in vain with their rifles ready. Below, a hail of artillery fire backs up the advance of Tenth Army troops. Despite fanatical resistance the Japs could not stop our troops from advancing to the northern tip of the island.

The Yanks make a second landing on Mindanao April 17, 1945

TROOPS MARCH INLAND. Following a sharp naval bombardment, troops of the Army's 24th Division were put ashore at Parang and Malabang on Mindanao by Navy landing craft. Opposition was light and after securing the beachhead this column began the march inland towards their first objective, the capital city of Cotabato, which was captured within three days.

THE WOUNDED WALK. Although suffering severe head wounds, a marine and a Navy hospital corpsman are able to go to the rear of the lines on their own power to receive further medical attention. After a comparative lull in the fighting on Okinawa a new general offensive was begun on April 19 and by the end of the month our troops had torn the Machinato airfield from the stubborn Japanese.

The Ninth rolls into Magdeburg

CITY IS SHATTERED. After furious fighting, the United States Ninth Army captured the important German city of Magdeburg on April 18. Troops of the Thirtieth Infantry Division are shown making their way through a pulverized street. On the American First Army front troops were in Leipzig; the Third Army was at the Czech border; the Seventh was fighting in Nuremberg.

The Japs go swimming in the China Sea

IT'S A LONG WAY TO JAPAN. Nipponese seamen struggle and cling to the side of their escort ship just before it plunged to the bottom of the China Sea near Amoy. The vessel was stricken by bombs of the Fifth Air Force. Note heads bobbing in sea.

Allied tanks in the ruins of Nuremberg

SHRINE CITY SURRENDERS.
On the evening of April 20, as hundreds of American tanks rolled into the bomb-shattered city, all enemy resistance ceased in Nuremberg. The surrender of this great city, one of the oldest in Germany, was a bitter blow to the Nazis inasmuch as it had been their chief shrine ever since they came to power. All the great party rallies had been held in the vast stadium which had been specially built for the purpose, while the city's chief square had been named the Adolf Hitler Platz. That square, like many other parts of Nuremberg, had suffered much destruction not only from Allied bombing but also from heavy artillery shelling made necessary by the last dogged resistance put up by picked S.S. defenders. Nuremberg had been a center of production for the German war machine, having many large engineering and electrical industries. Most of these factories had been destroyed by the day and night attacks carried out by the Anglo-American air forces. On April 21 about 14,000 prisoners of war were liberated in the Nuremberg area. The picture shows American tanks progressing at slow pace through the rubble heaps that were once the streets of Nuremberg.

REDS ENTER THE GERMAN CAPITAL. Soviet signalmen string a communication wire across the Spree River, above, and artillerymen shell a suburb, below. The heart of Germany broke only after enormous pressure was exerted by the Red armies at Frankfurt and Kuestrin on the Oder. From that point until the Russians reached the center of the city they had to fight every inch of the way.

POPULACE IS JUBILANT. For many months the Allies had battered at the German defenses below Bologna, Italy, but it was not until the April offensive of 1945 that the strongpoint fell. Here, American troops of the Thirty-fourth Division are completely surrounded by civilians as they parade through the streets with flags and banners. The last of the mountain barriers southwest of the city had also been breached and the American Fifth Army was surging into the Po Valley. The British Eighth Army was pushing up the Adriatic coast toward Ferrara, only eight miles distant.

PLACE FOR 6 PERSON

TOUR GERMANY. A committee of American legislators went to Germany at the request of General Dwight D. Eisenhower, to inquire into atrocity stories on the spot. Inspecting Buchenwald concentration Camp, above, are, left to right, Lieut. Gen. Hoyt S. Vandenberg, U. S. Ninth Air Force commander; Rep. John C. Kunkel of Pennsylvania; Rep. Leonard Hall, New York; and Rep. Claire Booth Luce, Connecticut. Below, Sen. Ernest W. MacFarland of Arizona and Sen. Burton K. Wheeler of Montana visit Berchtesgaden.

HANDS ACROSS THE ELBE. Soldiers of the United States First Army and the Russian First Ukrainian Army shake hands on a wrecked bridge at Torgau on the Elbe River where patrols of the two armies made their first historic meeting on April 25. General Courtney H. Hodges' men had come 700 miles from the Normandy beachhead and Marshal Ivan S. Koneff's men had come 1,400 miles from Stalingrad to cut the common enemy in two in the heart of Germany.

BANNERS ARE UNITED. Carrying their respective flags, victorious troops of the American and Russian armies march together along the Elbe River following their historic link-up there. Major General Emil F. Reinhardt, commanding the American 69th Division (third from right), chats with Major General Rusakov, commanding the Soviet 58th Guards Division. In the close-up below, the two leaders shake hands warmly and smile their satisfaction. The east and west now formed a common front and the doom of Germany was sealed.

SALUTE TO VICTORY. As Russian and American soldiers fraternized at the front, above, the Soviet home front saluted them in Moscow with a gigantic display of fireworks, 324 anti-aircraft guns shooting round after round of green, yellow, red and orange balls of fire into the sky. Marshal Stalin exclaimed jubilantly, "Long live the victory of the freedom-loving nations over Germany!"

EYE TO EYE. American troops brought with them many strange gadgets which aroused the curiosity of the natives of Okinawa. Here, a child stares with baleful fascination into the eye of a modern camera. The machinery of modern war must have amazed the natives even more—to say nothing of the Jap troops.

G. I.s TAKE OVER. The Eagle's Nest atop Obersalzburg Mountain in the Bavarian Alps, where Hitler in one of his intuitive moods decided to attack Russia, becomes a rest lounge for American soldiers shown at their ease while one man stands guard in the window. Battle-weary Yanks of the 101st Airborne Division boated, fished, took sun baths, and rode horses in Hitler's former playground.

NORTH ATLANTIC OCEAN

NORTH SEA

SHETLAND IS.

HEBRIDES

ORKNEY IS.

NORWAY

OSLO

SWEDEN

IRELAND

NORTHERN IRELAND

DUBLIN

GREAT BRITAIN

JUNCTION OF AMERICAN AND RUSSIAN ARMIES APRIL 26, 1945

DENMARK

COPENHAGEN

BALTIC

LONDON

Hamburg

Stettin

RUS. INTO B

AMSTERDAM

Dunkerque

HOLLAND

ELBE R.

BERLIN

ENGLISH CHANNEL

Cherbourg

Le Havre

BELGIUM BRUSSELS

GERMANY

Remagen

ODER R.

Brest

PARIS

665 MI.

LUX.

Metz

RHINE R.

Prague

CZECHOSL

Lorient

St. Nazaire

LOIRE R.

SEINE R.

DANUBE R.

Munich

D-DAY ALLIES INVADE EUROPE JUNE 6, 1944

Nantes

FRANCE

VIENNA

AUSTRIA

BU

Bordeaux

Lyon

SWITZERLAND

HUNGA

GARONNE R.

RHONE R.

Milan

PO R.

Venice

Turin

Marseille

ITALIAN LINE CRACKS APRIL 1945

Florence

ADRIATIC SEA

YUGOSLAV

BELGRA

SPAIN

ITALY

ROME

CORSICA

TYRRHENIAN SEA

ALBANIA

BALEARIC IS.

SARDINIA

Naples

Salerno

MEDITERRANEAN SEA

April 26, 1945

Legend

PEAK OF AXIS OCCUPIED AND CONTROLLED TERRITORY.

GERMAN-HELD AREAS AS OF APRIL 26, 1945.

NEUTRAL AND UNINVADED TERRITORY.

MILES 0 100 200 300 400

FINLAND

LAKE ONEGA

LAKE LADOGA

INKI

LENINGRAD

TALLINN

ESTONIA

RIGA

T.VIA

ANIA

UNAS

POLAND

AY 945

AW

lin

Lwow

Minsk

Smolensk

Orel

Kursk

MOSCOW

VOLGA R.

LIMIT OF GERMAN PENETRATION INTO RUSSIA

RUSSIA

Gorki

Kazan

Kuibyshev

Saratov

VOLGA R.

RUSSIANS WIN DECISIVE BATTLE OF STALINGRAD FEB. 2, 1943

1375 MI.

KIEV

Kharkov

STALINGRAD

DNIEPER R.

DNIESTER R.

Odessa

Rostov

Astrakhan

CASPIAN SEA

OMANIA

CRIMEA

Sevastopol

Krasnodar

Mozdok

BUCHAREST

DANUBE R.

B L A C K   S E A

Batum

BULGARIA

CE

BOSPORUS

Istanbul

ANKARA

T U R K E Y

Canarina

1911

LIMBER UP FOR PACIFIC DUTIES. Scrapping members of the Marine Corps Women's Reserve not only keep themselves in fighting trim but also give their sister marines a laugh. They're on board a Coast Guard manned troop transport in the South Pacific. Before shipping out for arduous overseas duty they were put through a leatherneck combat training course, below. The marines performed highly useful services in the combat zones just as did their prototypes in the Waves and Wacs.

NAZI CAPTIVES MARCH OUT. As Soviet tanks and infantry fight their way into the Berlinerstrasse, above, German war prisoners straggle in the opposite direction, below. The population of the capital was in a state of panic, a wave of suicides was reported, civilians and deserters were fleeing the Russians to join the Americans. Berlin was completely cut off, her fanatical defenders compressed in an area of the few square miles in the center of the battered city.

SS WOMEN CRACKED THE WHIP. In addition to male officials, these husky, well fed women were guards at the concentration camp at Belsen, Germany, which was captured by the British Second Army. Below, a communal grave at the camp overflows with the pitiful remains of prisoners who could not survive. Other living prisoners were found in a state of starvation and disease scarcely human.

HORRORS OF BELSEN CAMP. The indescribable scenes of horror, mass cruelty and degradation revealed in the huge concentration camp at Belsen shocked the civilized world. When the camp was overrun by the British Second Army more than 60,000 civilians, suffering from typhus and other diseases, were found herded together here. Hundreds were dying every day in the overcrowded huts and many of the living were too weak to be removed. Many of the inmates had been disfigured for life by continuous beatings and prolonged suffering. Above: children starved to death at Belsen.

RUSSIAN GUNS CRUMBLE DEFENSES. Suburb after suburb, street after street, fell before the inexorable advance of the mighty Red Army into the German capital. The First White Russian Army broke into Berlin from the east and the First Ukrainian Army pushed in from the south. A Soviet self-propelled gun clears a street, above, and a battery of mortars goes into action, below.

A Jap "Judy" misses the boat

BUT IT'S A CLOSE SHAVE. Streaking from the sky in a mad effort to crash against a Navy aircraft carrier, this Jap suicide plane skims past its target by a few feet and plunges harmlessly into the sea. The plane (in circle) was caught by the camera as it was outlined against the expensive carrier, loaded with Navy planes. In the picture below, another Judy misses its mark and careens into the ocean.

REDS GIVE THE ORDERS. In the German town of Ruegenwalde the Soviet military commandant takes over the keys to local enterprises and warehouses. Two frightened looking officials stand stiffly before their new boss, above, to give up the keys. In Landsberg, below, a Soviet patrol checks the documents of an anxious looking citizen of the Reich.

PANIC SPREADS. As the Allied juggernaut plunged into Germany, civilians raided supply sources left behind by the fleeing German armies. Here, men and women at Kulmbach ransack an abandoned freight car. However, as the Allies captured town after town they imposed rigid military discipline and looting was stopped. Also a non-fraternizing rule was placed on Allied troops.

FALLS TO THE FIFTH ARMY. Only twenty days after the start of the Spring offensive in Italy, L
Gen. Lucian K. Truscott's forces rolled into Milan, capital of Lombardy and birthplace of Italian fasc
Here, the First Armored Division approaches the city's famous cathedral. At the same time, the Ei
Army captured ancient Venice and rolled on virtually unchecked as the Nazis crumbled everywł

MUNICH FALLS TO SEVENTH. In its speedy march on the German southern redoubt area, the United States Seventh Army advanced 20 miles in one day to penetrate Munich, birthplace of Nazism. Here, doughboys parade triumphantly past the notorious beer cellar where Hitler made his abortive pusch in 1923 and where he was almost blown to bits by a bomb in 1939.

Mussolini and mistress are hung by their heels

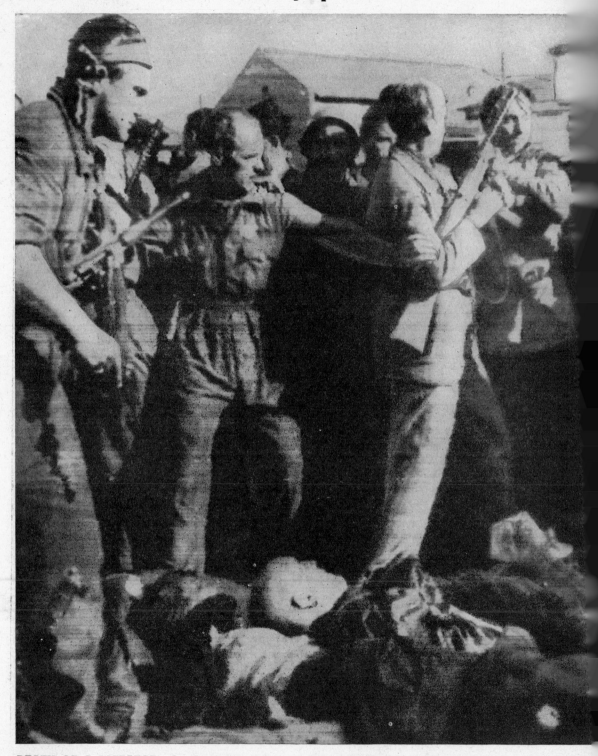

DEATH OF A DICTATOR. On April 28 a group of Italian Partisans summarily tried and executed Benito Mussolini and his mistress, Clara Petacci, along with twelve others at Lake Como. The dead bodies were piled on the floor of a moving van and driven to a public square in Milan, above, where a mad mob is shown trying to get at the former Dictator and his mistress who lies beside him. Several

of the mob succeeded in breaking through and kicking and maltreating the bodies after which they strung the disfigured corpses of Mussolini and Signorina Petacci, picture at right, by their heels in front of a filling station. Mussolini's executors reported that he died badly, crying out at the last, "No! No!" The grisly and lamentable mutilation of his corpse was decried by the Vatican.

1,000,000 NAZIS SURRENDER. Lieut. Gen. W. D. Morgan, Chief of staff to Field Marshal Sir Harold L. G. Alexander, lays down unconditional surrender terms to representatives of Col. Gen. Heinrich von Vietinghoff-Scheel and SS General Karl Wolff. The German representatives are in civilian clothes at extreme left in the above picture and General Morgan stands with his hands behind back, at right. The Germans agreed to lay down their arms on May 2 thus ending the war in Italy just twenty months after Italian soil was invaded by the Allies. The surrender came 14 days after the Fifth Army had started its spring offensive and 21 days after the Eighth Army had begun its drive, both armies sweeping over every important city in northern Italy and closing the Alpine passes. The lower picture shows General Morgan affixing his signature to the surrender instrument.

SPLIT JAPS. Tarakan, an island off the northeast coast of Borneo, was invaded by the Royal Netherlands Indies Army and Australian troops on April 30. The top picture shows the scarred landing beach at Lingkas. The oil well, below, was destroyed by the Dutch before the Japanese took the island in January, 1942. Recapture of the strategic territory meant an important air base for the Allies and also effectively severed the enemy forces in the south, isolating the Japs in the Netherlands East Indies.

LEADERS CONFER. Field Marshal Sir Bernard L. Montgomery, left, commander of the 21st Army Group, and Marshal Konstantin Rokossovsky, center, commander of the Second White Russian Army, leave the British Sixth Airborne Division command post at Wismar, Germany, where their troops joined for the first time, 62 miles northwest of Berlin.

A FUTURE FOR V-2? These German scientists gave themselves up to the United States Seventh Army in the Bavarian Alps where they were operating a V-2 experimental laboratory. They told interviewers that the V-2 bomb would shape "the course of the next war." Left to right, they are: Maj. Gen. Walter Dornberger, commander of the V-2 laboratory; Lieut. Col. Berbert Axter, scientist; Professor Wernther von Braun, inventor of the V-2 rocket; and Hans Lindenberg, scientist. Auto crash caused arm injury.

DOENITZ TAKES OVER. A German radio broadcast from Hamburg on May 1 startled the world with the announcement that Adolph Hitler had given his life in the defense of Berlin. Allied leaders were skeptical and wanted to see the body, but no trace was found. Contradictory stories of his mysterious death only confused the issue. Grand Admiral Karl Doenitz, a 53 year old U-boat specialist, stepped into the breach, proclaiming himself the new Fuehrer. Hitler, left, and Doenitz are shown here as they appeared together in 1942.

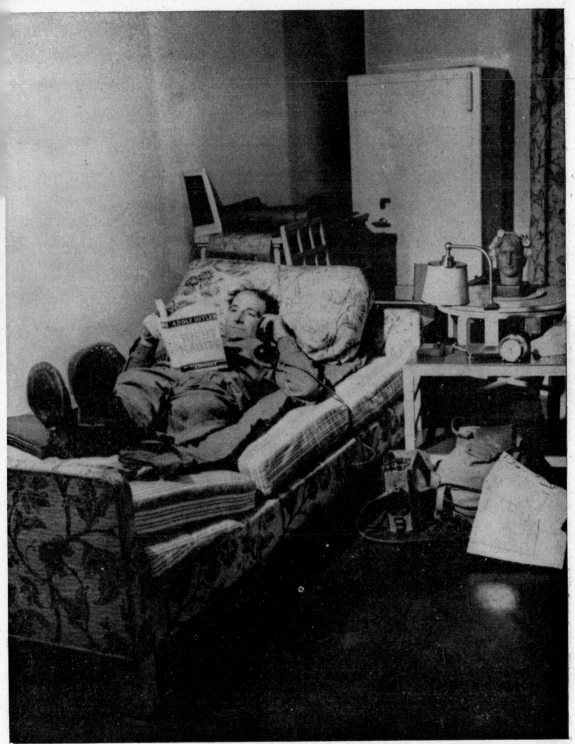

NOT AT HOME. Whether Hitler actually died in Berlin or "took it on the lam" doesn't make the slightest bit of difference to this G.I. Joe who makes himself comfy in the Fuehrer's bedroom at the Brown House, Munich. The new Fuehrer, Grand Admiral Karl Doenitz, said that the war would continue and it did— for a week. Later, the Allies imprisoned Doenitz.

ATTACK FROM THE NORTH. Troops of the Fourteenth Army raced toward Rangoon from the Meiktila-Prome arc in the north to join with other forces from the south. Sikh infantry clears the brush at bayonet point, above, and armored and ground troops push forward, below.

DROP FROM RAF PLANES. Culminating a 1,000 mile battle over mountains and jungle from Lashio and Kohima, British and Indian forces took Rangoon on May 3, attacking from land, sea and air. The first force into enemy territory at Rangoon was the Indian Parachute Regiment shown here. Simultaneously General Slim's 14th Army bore down from the north and seaborne landings were made by the Navy.

TROOPS CELEBRATE IN GENOA. Victorious Fifth Army troops move through the streets of Genoa, Italy, as civilian crowds come out to view them. It had been a very tough fight in Italy; Salerno and Cassino would not soon be forgotten. The American Fifth and British Eighth armies fought for many bitter months below Bologna before the sudden breakthrough.

ASSAULT RIVER MOUTH. Allied troops in barges from the British Navy forced the Rangoon river mouth twenty miles below the city after Indian and British paratroops had cleared the way a day earlier. Amphibious forces approach landing points, above, and wade ashore, below. Rangoon fell under combined sea, air and land blows on May 3.

IN THE CENTER OF THE CITY. On May 2, Berlin, greatest city of the European continent capitulated to the Russians after twelve days of deadly street fighting. Simultaneously Marshal Stalin announced the destruction of the German Ninth Army southeast of Berlin with the capture of 120,000 men and the slaughter of 60,000. The top picture shows the heart of Berlin in ruin; the lower picture shows the Friedrichstrasse where the last furious battle took place before the Germans quit.

ONLY A SHELL REMAINS. Molen-Markt Square still burns, above, and dazed civilians wander aimlessly through the wrecked streets of what was once the world's fourth largest city with a population of 4,335,000. Below, some of the 70,000 German troops that surrendered march through a devastated street. The futile defense of Berlin cost the city some 343,000 casualties in all, it was estimated.

NOT AT HOME. When Soviet soldiers entered the Reichs Chancellery in Berlin Hitler was not there to receive them. The building where the Fuehrer had hatched so many diabolical plots was wrecked and vacant, containing no trace of its former tenant. In these pictures, Russian soldiers wander at will in the shattered corridors from which the Nazis once controlled Europe.

AUTHOR OF THE BELGIAN BULGE. Field Marshal Karl von Runstedt, left, who schemed the abortive Battle of the Bulge in Belgium, was captured at his Bavarian retreat by soldiers of the American Seventh Army. With him are his son, center, Lieutenant Hans von Runstedt, and a medical attendant. The Marshal was formerly Supreme German Commander on the Western Front.

THE END OF A DIRTY BUSINESS. The Tenth Mountain Division saw as tough going as any in Italy and when the shooting stopped the battle-hardened troops gathered the following day at Torboli for prayer and thanksgiving. Here, the men bow their heads as their chaplain conducts them in solemn services.

BURMA CAMPAIGN VIRTUALLY OVER. With the capture of the capital city of Rangoon by the British Fourteenth Army the three year campaign to clear the Japs from Burma was virually at an end. Admiral Lord Louis Mountbatten declared that the Allies had inflicted 347,000 casualties on the Japanese in Burma (97,000 of them counted dead) and there was left to accomplish mopping-up operations only in Arakan and in a few sectors of the Irrawaddy delta. Rangoon was seized after troops had traversed 1,000 miles of mountains and jungles from Lashio and Kohima, winning the key city only ten days before the rains and storms of the monsoon were due to strike. Rangoon, third largest port on the Indian Ocean, had a pre-war population of 400,000 and was the hub of the Burma transportation system. The capture of the city, climaxing the Burma campaign, was effected by Chinese, American, British, Indian and African forces. The picture shows an R.A.F. regiment moving through a street in Rangoon

MUST CLEAN UP OWN MESS. When the fighting stopped in Berlin the troubles of the inhabitants were far from over. There remained the immense task of reconstruction—a job to be done by those who started the shooting. Here German men and women begin to shovel the vast ruin of their city. Even before other Allied occupation troops entered the city, the Russians put the Berliners to work.

MONTY LAYS DOWN TERMS.
On May 4 in an ordinary army tent at Luneburg Heath, near Hamburg, Field Marshal Sir Bernard Montgomery reads ultimatum for the surrender of German land, sea and air forces in northern Germany, Holland and Denmark. Hearing the terms (seated, facing camera) are Kontur Admiral Wagner, naval liason, and Gen. Admiral Hans Georg Friedeburg. General of the Infantry Kunzel, in the picture below, signs the surrender document as Field Marshal Montgomery looks sternly on. This mass surrender in the north delivered more than 1,000,000 German soldiers into the hands of the Allies, closing hostilities for the Canadian Army fighting in Holland, and the British Second Army fighting in Germany.

FORTY SUBS CAPTURED. When units of the 95th Infantry Division moved into the sector around Bremen, many U-boats were caught on the ways at Werfthafen in Bremen Harbor. This drydock, one of Germany's largest, held at the time 40 submarines, some of which are shown here in the various stages of repair and construction. When the war ended, German U-boats began to surrender at sea.

SENSIBLE JAPS. A group of Nipponese soldiers, tired of the fight, climb out of the rocks and bushes of one of the islands of Kerama Retto, near Okinawa, to give themselves up to the crew of a picket boat. In their bundles they carried money, razors, diaries, toilet articles, photographs and cigarette holders. There were no mass surrenders in the Pacific but as time went on more and more of the Japs seemed willing to give up rather than hazard the doubtful reward of dying for the Emperor in Samurai fashion. The full dinner pail, below, had far more charm for these Japs than the honors paid the dead in distant Japan. American propaganda leaflets as well as American power seemed to be having a growing effect on the Bushido spirit.

Germany surrenders unconditionally at Reims

NAZI COLLAPSE IS COMPLETE. The rapidly disintegrating Reich, most of it already overrun and defeated, capitulated formally in a little red school house at Reims, France at 2:41 A. M. French time on May 7 (May 6, 8:41 P. M. Eastern War Time) after five years, eight months and six days of bloodshed and destruction. The general scene of the surrender, upper left, shows the delegates of the victors and the vanquished coming to terms. With their backs to the camera are, left to right, Gen. Admiral Hans Georg Friedeburg, Commander in Chief of the German Navy; Col. Gen. Gustav Jodl, Chief of Staff of the German Army; and Maj. Gen. Wilhelm Oxenius, an aide to General Jodl. Facing the camera, seated,

left to right, are: Lieut. Gen. Sir F. E. Morgan, staff deputy; General Francois Sevez, representing France; Admiral H. M. Burrough, commanding naval Allied Expeditionary Forces; Lieut. Gen. Walter Bedell Smith, Chief of Staff to General Eisenhower; Lieut. Gen. Ivan Chermiaeff and General Ivan Susloparoff, Russia; Lieut. Gen. Carl A. Spaatz, Commanding General, U. S. Tactical and Strategic Air Force; and Air Marshal J. K. Robb, Deputy Chief of Staff (SHAEF). In the picture, upper right, Lieut. Gen. Smith signs the surrender for the Supreme Allied Command; lower left, Col. Gen. Jodl signs for Germany; lower right, General Susloparoff signs for the Soviet Union.

General "Ike" flashes a victory smile

HIS JOB IS DONE. The surre▮ der negotiations were carrie▮ out at General Dwight I▮ Eisenhower's headquarters ▮ Reims, but the general did n▮ himself meet with the delegate▮ Afterwards, however, he re▮ ceived General Jodl and Gen▮ Adm. Friedeburg to ask the▮ sternly if they understood th▮ terms of the surrender. With hi▮ great task successfully accom▮ plished, General "Ike" can af▮ ford to take a cigarette and smile his satisfaction, above. In the picture below, he and the Russian General Susloparoff "shake" and extend mutual congratulations as Lieut. Gen. Ivan Chermiaeff, left, grins appreciatively.

KEITEL SIGNS. Marshal Wilhelm Keitel, German Army commander, above, signs ratified surrender terms at Russian headquarters in Berlin on May 9. Sword of the rigid and correct general rests on the conference table. Below, the papers are checked over by Air Chief Marshal Sir Arthur Tedder, left, and Field Marshal Gregory K. Zhukov, Deputy Commander of all Soviet forces.

TWO TOKENS. Field Marshal Keitel raises his sword in a token of submission after signing ratification of unconditional surrender. With him are Col. Gen. Paul Stumpff, Luftwaffe commander, left, and Gen. Adm. Friedeburg, behind his shoulder. Below, a quite different symbol is raised as a toast is drunk to victory by, left to right, Air Chief Tedder, Marshal Zhukov and General Carl Spaatz.

"THE FLAGS OF FREEDOM FLY OVER ALL EUROPE." These were the solemn words of President Harry S. Truman as he announced to the nation the unconditional surrender of Germany. "The West is free," he said, "but the East is still in bondage to the treacherous tyranny of the Japanese." Meanwhile, in London, Prime Minister Winston Churchill declared that "the evildoers . . . are now prostrate before us." In the picture above, smiling President Truman announces to the press the complete victory of the Allies over Germany and, below, the Prime Minister waves his hat to cheering throngs in Whitehall. Behind him is Minister of Labor Ernest Bevin, left. Behind the President are Mrs. Truman and Mary Margaret Truman, while notables are seated along the wall.

V-E Day—New York, London, Paris

SYMBOLS OF VICTORY. Under the torch of the Statue of Liberty in Times Square, New York (picture at left), crowds riotously express their jubilation over victory in Europe. In the picture at the top, right, the royal family waves to cheering crowds at Buckingham Palace. Queen Elizabeth and King George are flanked by Princess Elizabeth, left, and Princess Margaret. Below, General Charles DeGaulle (facing camera, left center) lustily leads Parisians in the singing of the national anthem.

JOY IN MOSCOW. Throughout the Soviet Union victory over Germany was celebrated after an early morning broadcast by Marshal Stalin. In Moscow tens of thousands of people gathered to sing and dance in Red Square where they are shown, top picture, tossing a British Tommy gleefully above the crowd. Many smaller Allies were equally joyful as in Rotterdam, below.

TWO REACTIONS. In the battle line at Okinawa, men of the fighting 77th Infantry Division listen with grim faces to the news of Germany's surrender. The war was far from over for them. A few minutes later they were back in the fighting, killing or being killed. Below, a Wac detachment in Kandy, Ceylon, passes in review in celebration of the war's end in Europe.

IT'S HIS TURN NOW. As Norway fell with the rest of the German-held lands, this member of the Quisling party found himself at the other end of a gun for a change. A member of Norway's "death-gang" holds an automatic carbine firmly in his back. Meanwhile, the traitor's boss, Vidkun Quisling, and six members of his cabinet were behind bars in Norwegian jails.

WAS TOP GENERAL. Smiling Field Marshal Albert Kesselring, left, formally surrendered his armies on May 10 to Maj. Gen. Maxwell D. Taylor, right, Commander of the 101st Airborne Division of the Seventh Army. Kesselring was the last supreme commander in the west. He was appointed to that post in March but a month later his command was divided.

ORDERED OFF HIS SHIP. Admiral Wilhelm Meendsen-Bohlken, commanding all the German surface fleet, lowers his head as Commander R. J. Richards, British naval officer in charge, right, informs him that he has twenty minutes to pack and get off his ship before being placed under arrest at Eckernforde.

T NO. 2 NAZI GIVES UP. Reichsmarshal Herman Wilhelm Goering, top Nazi after Hitler, was seized
May 8 by Lieut. Gen. Alexander M. Patche's American Seventh Army. The rotund Nazi is shown
iling craftily, sweating, and bluffing (above) as he faced a battery of newspapermen May 11. Seized
with Goering were his actress wife and six-year-old daughter.

The U.S.S. Bunker Hill—a ship that wouldn't go down

SAVED BY MAN'S COURAGE. Fighting suffocating flames and exploding bombs, the gallant crew of the U.S.S. Bunker Hill sacrificed 392 dead or missing and 264 wounded to save their ship after it was struck by two Jap Kamikazes near Okinawa. The 27,000 ton carrier had sent her planes against Jap strongholds for 58 consecutive days before she was struck by two Jap suicide planes within 30 seconds of each other on the morning of May 11. The two planes released 500 pound bombs, which crashed through the flight decks, before making their suicide crashes into the vessel. The Bunker Hill's planes caught fire on the flight deck and the ship was swept by an inferno of exploding bombs and burning gasoline. As the crew fought the flames valiantly, the cruiser U.S.S. Wilkes-Barre and the destroyers Stembel, Charles S. Sperry, and English came alongside to help. As the ship listed more and more, Captain George A. Seitz made a decision which decided the fate of the Bunker Hill. Slowly, he had the big ship make a 70 degree turn. This shifted the load of water across the ship from starboard to port, literally dumping the heart of the inferno on the hangar deck into the sea. Later the Bunker Hill came home to the States, second only to the carrier Franklin as a surviving casualty of the war.

BATTLE INFERNO. Crewmen of the U.S.S. Bunker Hill stand amid the wreckage of planes and pour water upon flaming gasoline and explosives. Below, a huge hole gapes in the flight deck where a 500 pound bomb ripped through and exploded before hitting the water.

FINAL TRIBUTE TO HEROES. The entire ship's complement assembles on the flight deck and superstructure of the U.S.S. Bunker Hill in a solemn memorial service for those who gave their lives to save their ship. Three hundred and seventy-three were killed, nineteen were missing, and 264 were wounded in the carrier's heroic fight against flames and explosion.

CHANGING THEIR MINDS. Civilians of Beckum, Germany, look at a display of pictures showing atrocities committed by Nazis. This is part of the program for showing the Germans the error of their ways. Note the smirk on the man at left and the smiles of the small children. In addition to poster displays, civilians were made to view moving pictures depicting Nazi atrocities.

SKYWRITING. Attacking a United States Navy task force off Kyushu, this Japanese bomber scored a miss with its bomb load and then was itself caught in the deadly fire of the task force. Bursting into flame, the stricken bomber traces a smoky path across the sky before plunging into the ocean below. In the lower right corner of the photograph is a battleship of the Iowa class.

THEY WANT TO GRADUATE. This Camp Vassar is located not in Poughkeepsie, New York, but in Salzwedel, Germany, and was used as a Displaced Persons Center by the Eighty-fourth Infantry Division. The camp was formerly used by the German Luftwaffe. A G.I. talks with one of the camp's interpreters. Various displaced nationalities in Germany were a major problem confronting the Allies.

PROWLING ENDS. The first enemy warship to strike its colors to the American forces since V-E Day, the German submarine U-858 ended its destructive career forty-four miles off Cape May, N. J., where she is seen being boarded by Navy personnel as a blimp hovers overhead and another Navy craft stands by at the right. In two and one-half years of roaming with the Nazis' undersea "wolfpack", the U-858 reputedly sank sixteen Allied ships.

INTO THE JAWS OF DEATH. The fighting was bitter and casualties high as troops advanced slowly over the difficult terrain, above, towards Naha. Through May 15 the Japs lost 46,505 dead and 1,038 prisoners. Through May 14 our land forces lost 3,781 dead, 17,004 wounded, 165 missing. In supporting the ground forces the Navy reported 900 killed, 2,746 wounded, 1,074 missing.

1966

EXPLODE OIL REFINERY. United States Army Air Force Superforts paid a visit to the Japanese home island of Honshu to blast the Otake oil refinery. These before-and-after photographs show the excellent results. The target, above, is shown completely obliterated by smoke and flame, below.

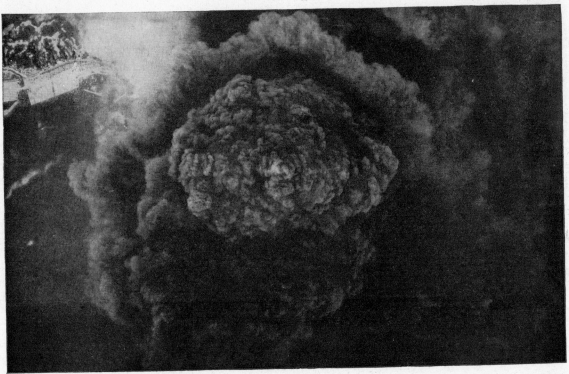

THE FLAG FLIES AT HALF MAST. Heroes of the Twentieth Bomber Command lie buried in this United States Military cemetery in the interior of China. The wounded Chinese soldier, below, was a victim of a Japanese mortar shell. Coordinated efforts of the American fliers and the Chinese ground forces were at last turning the tide in China, smashing the Japanese attack on the American air base at Chihkiang and crumbling the entire Japanese line in western Hunan Province. Reports claimed that more than 20,000 Japanese were killed in ten days on the Chihkiang front, threatening to oust the Japs from the Chinese interior.

NIPS ARE BLOWN FROM CAVES. Demolition and flame-throwing squads had to blast and sear the tenacious Japs from the caves strewing the ridges and hills before Naha. Leather-necks of the Sixth Marine Division, above, calmly watch as one of their dynamite charges violently eliminates Japs who insisted on remaining in a cave to join their ancestors. Below, a flame-throwing tank pours fire into the holes of a hillside where the fanatical Japs dug them-selves in.

CAUGHT NEAR BERCHTESGADEN. Unshaven and unkempt Dr. Robert Ley, 55-year-old Nazi labor leader, was captured in a mountain hideaway by troops of the 101st Airborne Division. The Yanks do not suppress their grins as the bedraggled Nazi pads by in thick-soled shoes. He wears an overcoat over pajamas.

Gestapo chief Himmler takes poison May 23, 1945

HE COULDN'T FACE THE MUSIC. After his apprehension by British guards at Bremervoerde, Hangman Heinrich Himmler decided that it was easier to die than to answer for his sins and he swallowed a capsule of cyanide poison which he had concealed in his mouth. The former head of the Gestapo should have known better, but he was captured because he was carrying fake discharge papers at a date when such papers were not being issued to the German Army. Picture at top shows also that he had shaved his mustache to disguise his identity. Another Nazi leader who couldn't take it was Gen. Adm. Hans Friedeburg, below, Commander-in-Chief of the German Navy and one of the signers of the unconditional surrender at Reims. He also swallowed poison.

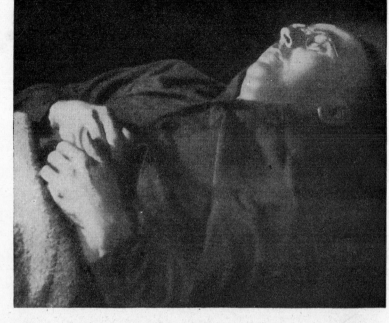

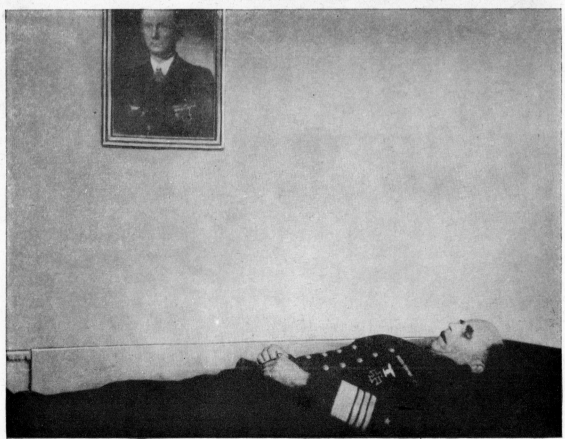

DRAFTED AT 80. This young fellow of 80 years saw service with the Military Railway Service of the U. S. Army in India. Able to push several loaded cars, he made it possible to do without a shunting engine at this siding near Ledo. This section of the Bengal railway was operated by the U. S. Army.

German civilians see horror movies

ONE CRIES, ANOTHER LAUGHS. When German civilians were made to view films of the horrors of Buchenwald and Belsen, one woman was moved, above, but another, below, laughed and is being sent back to view the picture a second time. Films were shown to the populace of Burgsteinfurt which was known as "The Village of Hate" because of its resentment of British occupation.

Britain's secret defense is revealed   May, 1945

A WALL OF FLAME WAS READY. After Germany was defeated authorities released the amazing story of a secret anti-invasion defense whereby the channel could be turned into a searing wall of fire almost instantly. Oil was piped to outer and inner defense lines in the channel where it could be ignited into sheets of roaring flame to repulse invasion forces. This picture shows the inner defense system during a test. Pools of oil are spreading over the water and are just beginning to burn. Within a few minutes an impregnable barrier of fire and smoke would rise from the water.

1974

GRAVEYARD WATCH. The many ridges and hills on Okinawa presented hazardous obstacles to troops on Okinawa and the advance was slow and bloody. In the above picture, marines pause in their advance across "Cemetery Ridge" as Jap bullets whistle overhead, temporarily pinning them down. The lower picture shows a First Division marine lining his sights on a Jap in the battle for Wana Ridge before the town of Shuri. The other leatherneck ducks warily for cover. As the month of May drew to a close the battles for Naha and Shuri, key points in the defense system of the Japs in southern Okinawa, were drawing to a climax with the Marines entering Naha and Army troops cracking Shuri's defenses.

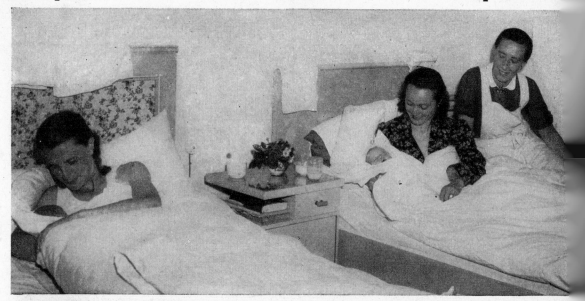

THE FUTURE—GERMAN STYLE. In the top picture two German mothers rest with their babies inside one of the German "Lying In" homes for both married and unwed. The woman at the left said, "My fiance is in the Army." The hospital, below, flaunts a flag, white with red center, which marks this and other similar centers, of which there are 15 in the Munich area.

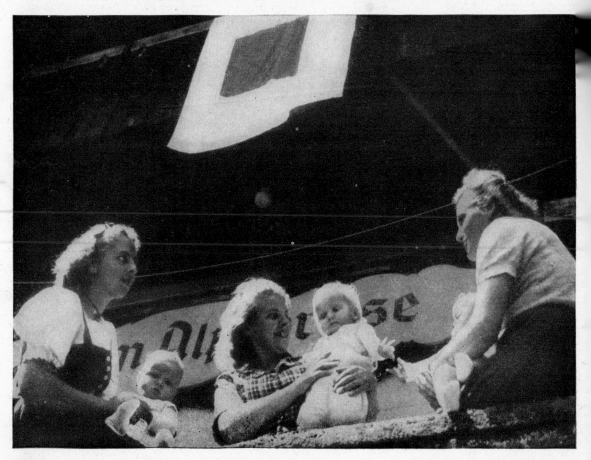

BOMB CRATER BATHTUB. Leathernecks bathe and wash their clothes in a bomb crater near a wrecked ap plane on Okinawa. In the picture below, the first Wacs to arrive in Manila, a few weeks earlier, make good use of an undamaged swimming pool which they discovered on the outskirts of the battered city in the Philippines.

PARAFRAGS RIP A RAILROAD. In the peaceful scene above, parafrags (parachuted bombs) floo
gently down upon the Chickunan railroad yard at Formosa. A moment later the bombs strike thei
target and explode, below, and parked trains and steel rails go up in a burst of destruction. Mediun
bombers of the Fifth Air Force made this mess of Jap transportation, under attack for many months

MEND SHIPS FAR FROM HOME. One of the biggest factors in Navy operations conducted far from major land bases is the floating dry dock or ASBD (advance base sectional dock). The ASBD, built in separate sections, is moved as close to the combat zone as possible. There, the sections are welded into one huge dock with a capacity of 56,000 to 100,000 tons, more than enough to raise our largest battleship. A battleship finds abundant room in the ten-section dry-dock in the picture at top. Below, however, the dock proves itself too wide for the Panama Canal, and Seabees, under the command of the Naval Civil Engineer Corps, tipped the mammoth dock on its side to pull it from one ocean to the other.

Arch traitors are rounded up

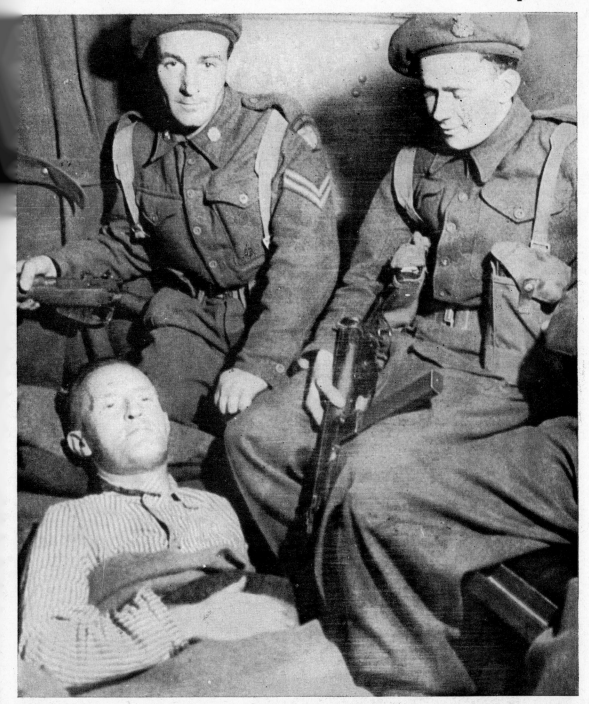

QUISLING AND JOYCE IN CAPTIVITY. On May 29 William Joyce, known as "Lord Haw Haw," was captured by troops of the British Second Army on the German-Danish frontier near Flensburg. When questioned, he made a movement with his right hand as if to draw a gun, and was promptly shot in the thigh. Joyce was then taken to Luneburg where the bullet was extracted, and shortly afterward was flown to England to stand trial. Throughout the war Joyce broadcast Nazi propaganda to Britain from Germany. He is seen above on an army stretcher soon after he was captured. During the same month the Norwegian traitor Vidkun Quisling was brought to justice at Oslo (he is seen in court on the opposite page). First of the major traitors of the war, he aided the Nazi invasion of Norway.

The end of a Jap Banzai charge

FANATICISM IS FUTILE. As the Yanks campaigned to rout out the last of the Japs on Mindanao, the Nipponese staged a Banzai charge near the Maramas airstrip with the result pictured here. Machine gun and rifle fire by Thirty-first Infantrymen mowed them down. The Yanks, who lost only two killed and seven wounded, stand in the background. The campaign to crush the remaining resistance on Mindanao was proceeding satisfactorily with our troops seizing Licanan airfield, fifteen miles north of Davao, and pushing quickly inland in the Davao region.

FRENCH AND ARABS CLASH.
Serious friction between the French and Arabs in Syria and Lebanon late in May brought about a crisis in the Levant which threatened the Allied lifeline to the Pacific from the Mediterranean. There was much bloodshed as French troops and natives fought. Damascus was shelled by the French (top cut shows damage) and the Syrian Parliament building, below, was wrecked. The situation became so hot that Prime Minister Churchill intervened with a sharp demand of General De Gaulle that hostilities cease. The French acceded to this demand and the fighting stopped, pending a settlement.

GRIM LEADERS SEE CAPITAL FALL. Taking up a front-line position during the storming of Naha, capital of Okinawa, Maj. Gen. Lemuel C. Shepherd, Jr. (holding walking stick), commander of the Sixth Marine Division, and Lieut. Gen. Simon Bolivar Buckner (holding camera), chief of the Tenth Army, watch their forces take the town. Later, on June 18, when General Buckner was watching the end of the Okinawa campaign, he was killed instantly by one of the last heavy shells fired by the Japs.

JAP STRONGHOLD FALLS. After fierce fighting, First Marine Division troops smashed into the Okinawa key position of Shuri, planting the stars and stripes over Shuri Castle, former enemy headquarters. Marine Lieut. Col. R. P. Ross, Jr., proudly affixes the flag on a ridge above the castle. Enemy tanks were thrown against the Marines north and east of the city in a vain effort to halt them.

1986

OSAKA BECOMES STEAMING CAULDRON. Smoke and flames boil skyward from Osaka after B-29 Superfortresses raided the second largest city and industrial center of Japan. The devastating incendiary attack set the entire water front ablaze. Four hundred and fifty B-29s dropped 3,200 tons of fire bombs; one hundred and fifty Mustangs escorted the Superfortresses.

1987

CRYBABY. America gave such a tremendous ovation to General George S. Patton, Jr., that he was carried away with emotion at a state dinner in Boston. The pistol packing hero of Africa and Europe weeps unashamedly. A great general in the field, he led the Third Army's lightning sweep through France and was a potent driving force in the final triumph over Nazi Germany.

DOWNED OFF OKINAWA. In the top picture, a curtain of steel is laid down by an American warship against an attacking Jap plane off Okinawa. The plane is coming head-on, just over the horizon but she hasn't a chance in the murderous hail of shrapnel. Below, a Nip plane attacking a flatop of the Essex class explodes in mid air after being hit by heavy AA guns. Destroyer in background joints fight.

DEATH VALLEY. Marines advance over the waste of a battlefield littered with enemy dead, as they seek hiding places of survivors who might menace their rear. One marine pauses reflectively by the bodies of the dead Japanese, while the others go forward under the gesticulated orders of the leader. One Jap has apparently been decapitated by a shell. Note also the stretcher on ground.

YANK PLANES SOFTEN OBJECTIVES. Australia's famed Ninth Division made a series of surprise landings on Borneo June 10 following heavy bombardments by American air forces and the Seventh Fleet. Venturas attached to the 13th Army Air Force Fighter Command made a shambles of Brunei Town, Borneo. Here, the papier mache town is shown in complete conflagration.

LANDINGS QUICKLY EFFECT-ED. The neck of this Jap Zero float plane was broken by an Allied naval shell before she could rise from the water at La-buan, Borneo, and the airstrip at Brunei, below, was heavily pocked from the air, making it impossible for Jap planes to oppose landings. The main assault on Labuan Island, just off the mainland of Borneo, resulted in the speedy capture of Victoria and the airfield. Another landing, on the mainland at Brooke-ton, made swift progress toward the town of Brunei. By this surprise stroke, the Allies straddled the Jap positions in the East Indies and achieved mastery of the southwest Pacific.

THE FINAL PHASE. Land, sea and air forces united to rout the last of the Japs from the southern tip of Okinawa in the final stage of the campaign. Here, a marine Corsair fighter looses a load of rocket projectiles against the southern ridges where the last-ditch Nips put up their final struggle. Waves of these planes kept up a continuous rocket barrage.

IT FAILS TO TURN THE TIDE. Many types of planes were used by the Japs in suicidal smashes at the Pacific Fleet but the Baka bomb shown here was the only plane specially designed for the purpose. Kamikaze or suicide pilots started to operate on a large scale for the first time at Leyte. The wave of Kamikazes reached its frenzied height during the three month battle of Okinawa. The suicide planes took a large toll of shipping and men but were unable to halt our advance towards the home islands and the heavy almost day and night naval and aerial fight for Okinawa ended in victory for the American forces, with many of the Kamikazes being "splashed" (lower picture).

GROGGY JAPS GIVE UP. A marine rifleman gives the cease fire order with his hand as a badly damaged Jap emerges from a cave on Okinawa, top picture. But, although the bitter Okinawa campaign was drawing to an end, the marines below took no chances when a bearded Jap offered to surrender. They gingerly search his clothing at arms length to make sure he isn't carrying a concealed weapon or a hidden explosive to sell his life for theirs. The Nips gave up in considerable numbers at the end of the battle for Okinawa, but they were still capable of fanaticism and treachery.

DIE BEFORE FIRING SQUADS. A Hitler youth, age 17 (top picture), is tied to a stake before his execution by an American firing squad. He was convicted with a companion of spying behind the American lines. Below, Ninth Army officers time a four minute interval after shooting to declare officially dead a German S.S. trooper, convicted of espionage in civilian clothing. He was one of six Germans shot near Braunschweig on June 14. Note coffins in background.

SAD FAREWELL. Colonel Francis I. Fenton, regimental commander in the First Marine Division, kneels bareheaded beside the flag-draped body of his son, Private Michael Fenton, who was killed in Okinawa. Father and son were in the same regiment. A few days later resistance was broken on Okinawa; Tenth Army casualties were 6,990 killed and missing, 29,598 wounded.

CONQUERING HERO. General Dwight D. Eisenhower, Supreme Allied Commander in Chief, was cheered by more than 1,000,000 Americans upon his return to the United States. He is shown giving the V-for-Victory sign at a Washington luncheon in his honor. The man who led the Allies to victory in Europe said that every soldier wanted peace but not until Japan was beaten.

FUTILE FLIGHT. By June 21 the enemy on Okinawa was driven into three small pockets on the southern tip of the island and there was no place to go but into the Pacific Ocean. This Jap, scuttling along the sea-wall, will soon meet the fate of his companion in the mud unless he surrenders. On June 19, 2,565 Nips had surrendered; 87,343 were killed.

"A VICTORY AGAINST WAR ITSELF." After nine weeks of deliberations to assure peace to the world, the historic United Nations Conference ended in San Francisco with a speech by President Truman and the signing of the Charter of the United Nations by the fifty nations present. Here, the Charter, designed for postwar peace, is signed by Secretary of State Edward R. Stettinius, Jr. The President looks on.

PENETRATE INDO-CHINA. Liuchow, former important American airbase in south-central China, was re-captured by Generalissimo Chiang Kai-shek's troops after a heavy assault lasting nearly a month. Chinese troops, above, and civilians, below, re-enter the burning city which the Japs had seized from the American Fourteenth Air Force in November, 1944.

Okinawans are evacuated to new village

MOVE FROM SOUTH OF ISLAND. Civilians in the south of Okinawa plod wearily along a dock to be taken by LST to a new village in the north under the supervision of the Military Government. The war was not nearly as tough on them, however, as it was on the marines, lower picture, who are resting after the bitter fighting at the close of the Okinawa campaign.

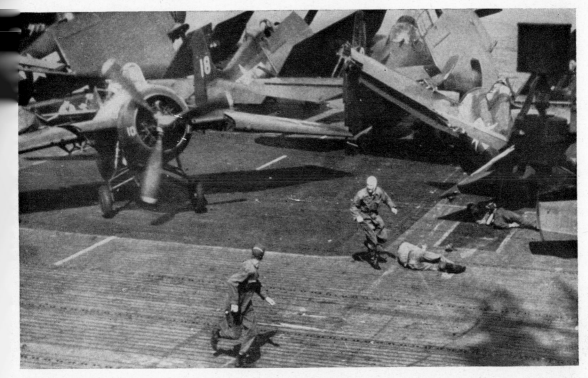

FRANKENSTEIN. Missing the arresting gear on a Pacific Fleet carrier, a plane returning from a mission against the Japs goes wild on the flightdeck as two crewmen run for cover and two others are knocked down, above. In the picture below, all four flightdeck crewmen roll on the deck to get away from the wildly flailing machine.

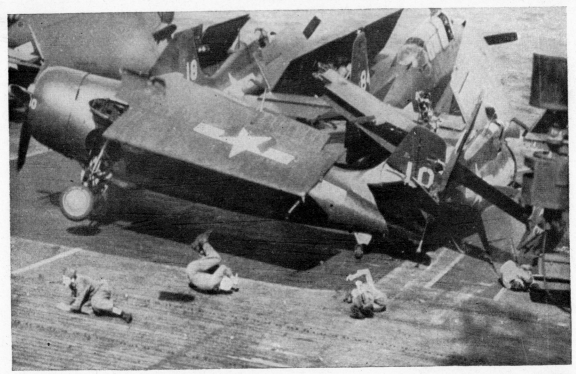

ENCOUNTER STIFF RESISTANCE. A terrific bombardment by 10,000 rockets from Seventh Fleet units struck installations at Balik Papan before Aussies of the veteran Seventh Division hit the beaches on July 1. The picture shows rockets hurtling towards the eastern Borneo shore while the Stars and Stripes wave proudly above the smoke of battle. The landings, conducted against stiff opposition, completed the rupture of Jap East Indies positions begun by the earlier invasions of Tarakan and Brunei. General MacArthur went ashore with his troops.

ORDEAL OF FIRE. The Japs clung so tenaciously to their caves and ditches that they frequently had to be burned out of hiding. As a last resort this Aussie, upper left corner, turns his flame-thrower into the hideout of a Jap on Borneo. The Nip emerges, his body a torch, and staggers in agony until the searing flames bring him writhing to the ground.

GUNS ON JAPAN. Big guns of the U. S. S. Massachusetts are trained directly on Kamaishi, important factory town on shore of Honshu, in first shelling of the Jap homeland by warships. Coordinated with this audacious attack, were more than 1,000 Third Fleet planes which rained destruction on Honshu and Hokkaido. Some of world's greatest warships were in attack on homeland.

CRACK-UP. A Jap freighter snaps in two when it is caught by a direct bomb hit east of Hokkaido. The damage was done by a carrier-based plane from the Third Fleet. An empty lifeboat can be seen at the top and center of the picture. The bow of the vessel broke away following an internal explosion. A streak of flame and a black billow of smoke gush skyward.

DISCUSS WAR AND PEACE. President Harry S. Truman, Marshal Stalin (left), and Prime Minister Churchill (right) opened their conference at Potsdam, in the outskirts of Berlin, to plan the peace in Europe and the final defeat of Japan. The newcomer to the Big Three was President Truman, who brought along his Secretary of State, James F. Byrnes, shown in the center of the lower picture chatting with the President and the skipper of the Augusta which made the journey across the Atlantic. The early days of the conference were shrouded in a security blackout but on July 27 the Potsdam ultimatum to Japan was given, reaffirming the principles of the Cairo Declaration: the end of militarism, punishment of war criminals, establishment of democracy and limitation of Japanese territory to the home islands. The conference ended August 2.

TOKYO NEXT. President Harry S. Truman, at microphone, with a group including Generals Patton and Bradley and Secretary of War Henry L. Stimson, watches the American flag as it is unfurled over the United States Group Control Council Headquarters in Berlin. Flag is the same that flew over the capitol in Washington D. C., when war was declared against the Axis on December 8. 1941.

BRITAIN CHANGES HORSES. In a stunning electoral landslide, Great Britain swung to the left, putting Labor into power with a smothering majority over the Conservatives who had held sway under Prime Minister Winston Churchill since May 11, 1940. Major Clement Richard Atlee immediately was elevated to power and formed a Laborite Government, appointing six well-known labor leaders to the new Cabinet, including Ernest Bevin as Foreign Secretary. "We have first of all to finish the war against Japan," declared Atlee. The new Prime Minister is shown with his wife, amidst cheering supporters.

PETAIN ON TRIAL. On July 23 the eighty-nine-year-old Marshal of France, Philippe Petain, head of the former Vichy Government, appeared at the Palais de Justice in Paris on a charge of treason. During the three-week trial evidence for the prosecution was given by famous French political leaders including two former premiers, M. Daladier and M. Reynaud. The traitor Pierre Laval appeared for the defense and is seen above giving his evidence while Petain listens. Petain was sentenced to death but the death penalty was commuted by General de Gaulle to imprisonment for life. Laval was later also tried and was sentenced and shot by a firing squad in October.

U.S. submarines help strangle Japan

SUBS TOTAL 1,256 "KILLS."
The Pacific submarine fleet, three craft of which are shown here, helped greatly to cut Japan's sea lifelines and to hasten her blockade and defeat. In the last three months of the Pacific war our underseas raiders accounted for sixty-nine Japanese ships sunk, bringing the total bag in the Pacific to an estimated 1,256 "kills." Vice Admiral Charles A. Lockwood, Jr., commander of the Pacific Fleet submarine task force, reported that many other ships were almost certainly sunk but could not be counted because of the strict standards set up for determining sinkings. In addition, he estimated that more than 300 other Japanese vessels were damaged.

THE NAVY REFUELS AT SEA. The vastness of the Pacific made it necessary for the Navy to perfect a technique for refueling at sea. Although the operation became routine, it was frequently hazardous as the vessels had to be brought alongside and kept alongside until the operation was complete, as shown in this picture. By this method warships could stay at sea for months.

ONE BOMB DEVASTATES HIROSHIMA. A gigantic pillar of smoke hurtled up into the stratosphere after a single atomic bomb was dropped on the important Japanese city of Hiroshima, utilized as an army depot and embarkation point by the foe. The smoke column climbs 20,000 feet from a 10,000 foot-wide dust cloud base. This cataclysm stunned the world; the end of the war was near; a new era at hand.

The dead city of Hiroshima

ATOMIC WASTELAND. Sixty percent of Hiroshima, a city of 318,000 inhabitants, was wiped out by the terrific force of the explosion of one atomic bomb equalling the force of 20,000 tons of TNT. Fifty thousand persons were reported killed, 55,000 wounded, and 200,000 homeless. This Japanese report may well be believed upon looking at this picture of incredible devastation. Only the skeleton of a church and one other building are left standing. Train service in the Hiroshima and other areas was suspended. President Truman stated, "The force from which the sun draws its power has been loosed against those who brought war to the Far East." Work on the bomb was the war's top secret and went by the name Manhattan Project. It was revealed that the enemy was also working frantically to perfect the terrible weapon first but, in the words of Churchill, "By God's mercy British and American science outpaced all German efforts."

THE MEN WHO BOMBED HIROSHIMA. Only three men aboard the B-29 that atom-bombed Hiroshima knew the nature of their world-shaking cargo. They were: Navy Capt. William S. Parsons (upper left), an ordnance expert; Major Thomas W. Ferebee (upper right), bombardier who dropped the bomb; and Col. Paul Tibbets, Jr. (lower picture), who piloted the Superfortress to its ill-fated target. There were several alternative targets in the area around Hiroshima but weather conditions "favored" the city of Hiroshima.

BIRTHPLACE OF ATOMIC BOMB. Work on the atomic bomb was a joint effort of British, Canadian, and American scientists and workers, but America was the site of the two billion dollar project to harness atomic energy. The work was done in three hidden cities by 100,000 workers. Two of the plants, one at Oak Ridge, Tennessee (above), and another at Richland, Washington (below), are pictured here.

COOPERATIVE ACHIEVEMENT. The epochal harnessing of atomic energy was the result of a gigantic pooling of effort and brains. Simply stated, the terrific force of the atomic or "cosmic" bomb was achieved by the splitting of the atom in a rare form of uranium and the setting up of a chain reaction. Many scientists contributed to the success of the Manhattan Project. Those scientists shown in the top picture are, left to right: Sir James Chadwick, of Great Britain; Maj. Gen. Leslie R. Groves, in charge of the project; Dr. Richard C. Tolman, of Office of Scientific Research and Development, Washington, D. C.; Dr. H. D. Smyth, project consultant, from Princeton, N. J. Bottom picture shows Professor Ernest Orlando Lawrence at the panel of cyclotron at University of California. Many others contributed to success of project.

LIGHTNING STRIKES AGAIN. A pillar of boiling smoke zooms through the clouds and mushrooms 20,000 feet above Nagasaki, second Japanese city to feel the terrible power of the atomic bomb—this time an improved version which authorities claimed would make the first bomb obsolete.

Devastated Nagasaki—prelude to peace

THE FINAL BLOW. Two days after Nagasaki was levelled by the second atomic bomb, Japan offered to surrender. The complete desolation of the port city is shown here as Jap workers carry away debris. Tens of thousands of people were killed, wounded and made homeless. Japanese reports that deadly radio-activity continued long after explosion were discredited by Allied authorities.

STRIKE AT MANCHURIA. The long-awaited entry of Russia into the war against Japan came at 12:01 o'clock on the morning of August 9. Soviet troops began hostilities along Manchuria's eastern front with Siberia just nine minutes after the declaration of war. The Red Army, operating on a wide front, quickly broke through heavy ferro-concrete fortifications like the one in the top picture and made gains up to fourteen miles. It crossed the Amur and Ussuri Rivers and captured many towns, including Hailar, bottom picture. The attack came just four days after the first atomic bomb fell upon Hiroshima and when Japan was already buckling on the brink of surrender.

TOKYO RADIO FLASHES NEWS. A Japanese offer to accept the Potsdam ultimatum with the proviso that the Emperor remain on his throne was flashed to the world by Domei, Japanese radio service, on August 10. A tense world was kept waiting until August 14 when the Japanese surrender offer was officially accepted by Washington. Between these dates rumors and counter-rumors kept the world agog.

EXCITEMENT RUNS HIGH. After the Domei flash that Japan was ready to surrender, crowds feverishly awaited official word from the White House. An incorrect radio flash announced the end on August 13 and the pent up people broke wild with premature celebrations. Here is a crowd watching the news bulletins in Times Square before the official end of the war—but paper already litters the street.

WORLD WAR II ENDS. President Truman reads the history-making Japanese surrender message to his cabinet and the long-drawn, bloody hostilities of World War II are over. Flanking the President at his desk are Admiral William D. Leahy, Secretary of State James F. Byrnes, and former Secretary of State Cordell Hull. Below, the President joins in a three-way handshake wtih Byrnes and Hull; all over the world millions of thankful people were praying and riotously celebrating. Official V-J Day had to wait for the formal signing of the surrender instrument and the war would not end technically until proclaimed by the President or by a joint resolution by Congress. But for the millions of people who had fought and suffered through the weary three years and 250 days following Pearl Harbor this day was the big one.

Pearl Harbor—at the end of Japanese war

VICTORY FIREWORKS. A display of fireworks quite different from that of December 7, 1941, lights the night of August 14, 1945, at Pearl Harbor. The infamy of Pearl Harbor was wiped clean by the complete victory over the foe which had struck so treacherously nearly four years before. Colored flares from every ship in the great naval base light the night sky. The unconditional surrender of Japan, with the Emperor taking orders from MacArthur, very clearly meant that Americans would not forget Pearl Harbor.

The victors and the vanquished

JOY AND SORROW. American sailors at Pearl Harbor go wild with joy and Japanese prisoners on Guam take their defeat bitterly as they listen with bowed heads to the news of surrender. American soldiers on Guam celebrated all night when the first Domei flash announced that Japan was ready to quit. In Manila there were also riotous reactions to the news. The Yanks let go with anti-aircraft barrages in the Philippine capital and several casualties resulted from their exuberance. Meanwhile Russian troops kept right on fighting the war in Manchuria where they made sweeping advances against almost no opposition.

ARRIVE AT IE SHIMA. Although it was relatively simple for Washington to accept the Jap surrender offer, it was a complicated matter to actually effect the surrender. A sixteen-man Jap surrender delegation arrived at Ie Shima, off Okinawa, on August 19. From there they were to fly to Manila where they would receive their instructions and give information which would enable the Allies and the Japanese to get together for signing of the formal instrument of surrender and for the intricate business of taking over the Nipponese Empire. The picture is a close-up of sour-faced Lieut. Gen. Takashiro Kawabe, head of the Jap delegation (left) and some of his aids.

"SHAKE, PAL." Lieut. General Takashiro Kawabe extended his hand upon arrival at Manila, but Col. S. F. Mashbir, official interpreter for American forces, catches himself in time and gestures with his hand, leaving the Jap's hand awkwardly grasping the air. Stern, correct, and businesslike deportment of the Americans soon put an end to the sudden hypocritical gestures of friendship by the Japs.

"SO SORRY. . ." One of the crewmen of the Jap plane which brought emissaries to Ie Shima en route to Manila stands furtively beside the plane with a bouquet of flowers which he brought from Japan as a token of "peace and friendship." Two of the emissaries hold their samurai swords, right, and American MPs in background keep an eye on them.

DELEGATES GET DOWN TO BUSINESS. General Kawabe, vice chief of the Imperial Staff and head of Nip surrender delegation, lowers his head and presents credentials from the Emperor to austere Lieut. Gen. Richard Sutherland, Chief of Staff to General MacArthur. In the picture below, tall Major Gen. C. A. Willoughby (left) leads General Kawabe and aides to their side of the conference table. The three Americans at the extreme right are, left to right: Major Gen. S. J. Chamberlain, General Sutherland, and Rear Admiral Sherman. The Jap armistice mission was called into a night session only three hours after their long and tiring flight from Tokyo. They returned to Tokyo after nineteen hours in which time they freely gave information for the effectuation of the surrender terms. Formal signing of the surrender papers was set for end of month.

Japanese Fifth Kwantung Army Group gives up

SURRENDERS TO SOVIET FORCES. Fighting on for days after the Jap bid for peace had been accepted, the Russians completely subjugated the Japanese Fifth Kwantung Army Group in Manchuria, rapidly disarming troops and seizing top commanders. In the picture across the top of these pages, the capitulation is negotiated by Marshal Vasilevsky (hands folded on table), who was in supreme command of the Far Eastern theater. At the right is Lieut. Gen. Hata, Chief of Staff of the Kwantung Army, and with Marshal Vasilevsky is Marshal Meretskov, commander of the First Far Eastern Front. In the picture at the left, Soviet sailors hoist the Red flag over Port Arthur, warm water port which the Russians lost to the Japs in the war of 1904-05.

MacArthur and his boys arrive in Japan

OCCUPATION BEGINS. The Yanks above (with interpreter) were among the first to land on Japanese soil when occupation operations began at Atsugi airfield on August 28. In the picture at the right, General MacArthur, Japan's new boss, is also with first arrivals at the airfield just outside of Tokyo. After the long, bloody fight from Australia the invasion of the home islands was without incident. It was the first time in one thousand years that foreign troops had occupied Japan. MacArthur told his men of the Eleventh Airborne Division that "From Melbourne to Tokyo was a long, hard road, but this looks like the payoff." Meanwhile, naval units were taking over in Tokyo Bay while Admiral Nimitz watched from the battleship South Dakota and Admiral Halsey's Third Fleet rode at anchor in the shadow of Mount Fujiyama.

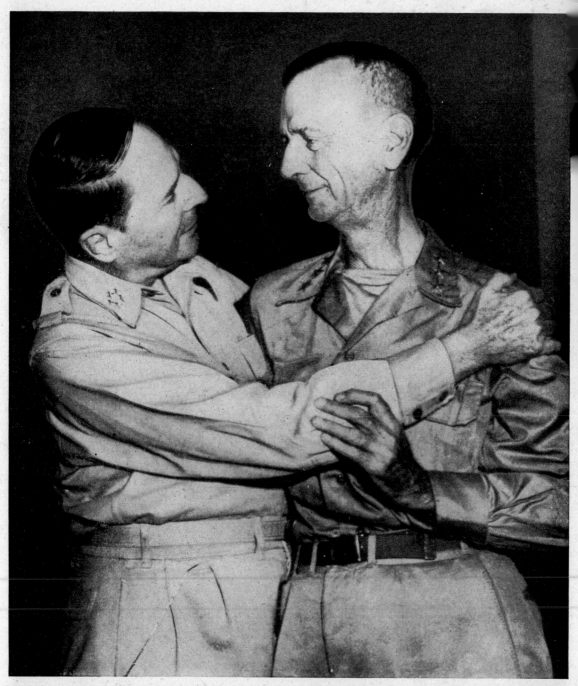

WAINWRIGHT RETURNS. "Oh, boy! This is what I've been hoping and waiting for for three and a half years. I couldn't be happier." So said Lieut. Gen. Jonathan M. Wainwright upon arriving in Yokohama after almost four years imprisonment by the Japs in Manchuria. Here, the gaunt general is embraced by his commander, General MacArthur (left) who left him in charge of the Philippines in May, 1942. MacArthur was ordered out of the Philippines to lead the Allied forces back from Australia. It was Wainwright's lot to finish a losing battle at Bataan. Wainwright stated: "My heartfelt gratitude goes out to the American people . . . for the generous and sympathetic understanding of the dire misfortune which befell me in the Philippines in May of 1942." The general received a hero's welcome.

TOKYO BAY FINALE. General of the Army Douglas MacArthur and Fleet Admiral Chester W. Nimitz stride across the deck of the U.S.S. Missouri to complete the final act of Japan's formal surrender. An aide precedes the two leaders and high officers of the Allied Command stand by at attention. The table is set for the signing of the instrument of surrender.

SHOWDOWN. General MacArthur, stepping to the microphone to direct the ceremony, turns to glance at his backing of representatives of the Allied Nations. They are, left to right, Lieut. Gen. Kuzma Nicolaevich Derevyanko, Soviet Union; General Sir Thomas Blamey, Australia; Col. L. Moore-Cosgrave, Canada; General Jacques Leclerc, France; Admiral C. E. L. Helfrich, Netherlands; and Vice Marshal Leonard M. Isitt (only partly visible), New Zealand. The United Kingdom representative, Admiral Sir Bruce Fraser,

is just out of the picture at the Soviet representative's right. The top-hatted and uniformed Japanese delegation stands stiffly at attention (right hand page). They are, left to right, Mamoru Shigemitsu, Jap foreign minister (top hat); Katsuo Okazaki, Central Liaison Office (top hat); General Yoshijiro Umezo; Rear Admiral Todatoshi Tomioka of Naval General Headquarters; Shunichi Kase, Government Information Bureau (top hat); right, Lieut. Gen. Shuichi Miyakazi, Army General Headquarters.

The Japanese Empire is signed away

THE PEN FOLLOWS THE SWORD. General Douglas MacArthur starts his signature on the surrender document with one of the five pens he used to complete name (left hand page). Behind MacArthur stand Lieut. Gen. Jonathan Wainwright, hero of Corregidor, and Lieut. Gen. A. E. Percival, British commander who was humiliated at Singapore. Mamoru Shigemitsu signs for the Japanese (picture at right) as American officers sternly watch him. By these signatures the fighting was formally ended, and President Truman proclaimed September 2 as V-J Day.

Japan at the end of the Second World War

THE PRICE OF AGGRESSION. By her ill-considered sneak attack on Pearl Harbor, December 7, 1941, Japan sought to dominate the orient, possibly the world, but after a period of initial successes which

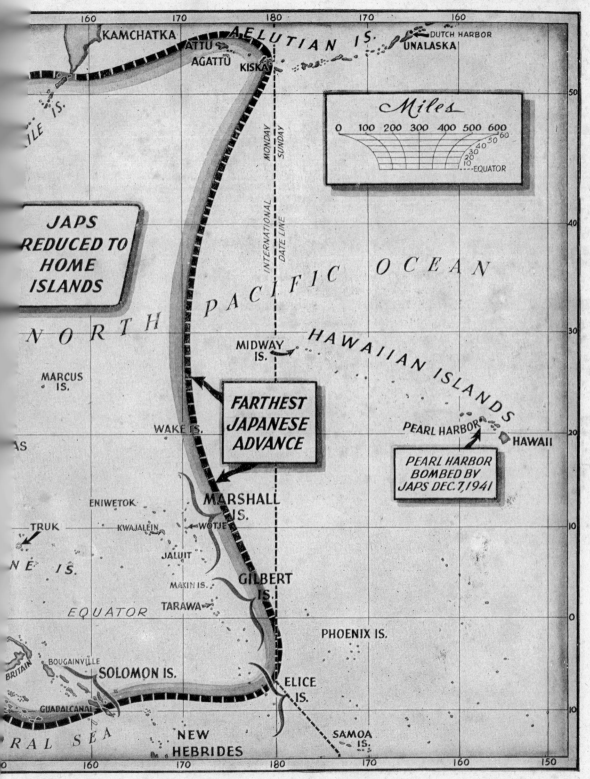

carried her to the outside circle on the map, she was forced back step by step, on land, sea and air, until her unconditional surrender squeezed her into the inner circle of her home islands.

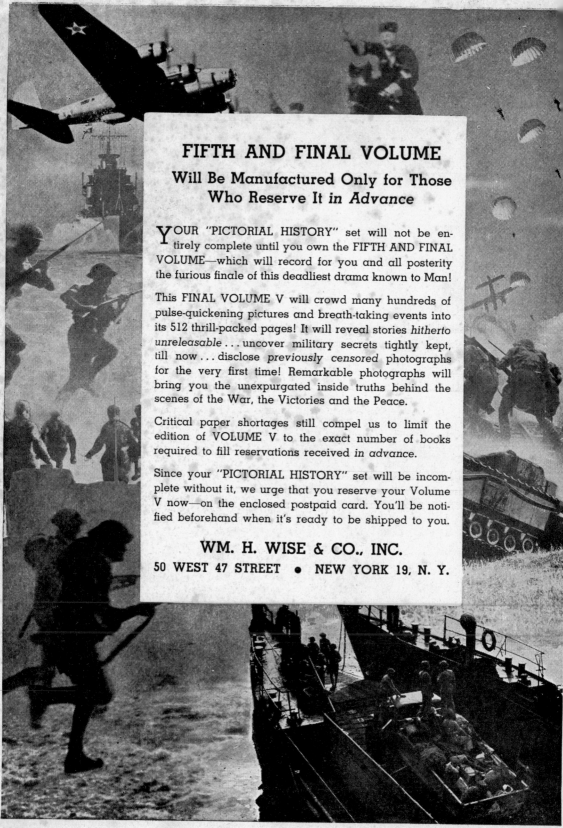

FIFTH AND FINAL VOLUME
Will Be Manufactured Only for Those Who Reserve It *in Advance*

Your "PICTORIAL HISTORY" set will not be entirely complete until you own the FIFTH AND FINAL VOLUME—which will record for you and all posterity the furious finale of this deadliest drama known to Man!

This FINAL VOLUME V will crowd many hundreds of pulse-quickening pictures and breath-taking events into its 512 thrill-packed pages! It will reveal stories *hitherto unreleasable* . . . uncover military secrets tightly kept, till now . . . disclose *previously censored* photographs for the very first time! Remarkable photographs will bring you the unexpurgated inside truths behind the scenes of the War, the Victories and the Peace.

Critical paper shortages still compel us to limit the edition of VOLUME V to the exact number of books required to fill reservations received *in advance*.

Since your "PICTORIAL HISTORY" set will be incomplete without it, we urge that you reserve your Volume V now—on the enclosed postpaid card. You'll be notified beforehand when it's ready to be shipped to you.

WM. H. WISE & CO., INC.
50 WEST 47 STREET • NEW YORK 19, N. Y.